HONEST SEX

HONEST SEX

A Passionate Path to Deepen Connection
and Keep Relationships Alive

Shana James, M.A.

NEW DEGREE PRESS

COPYRIGHT © 2022 SHANA JAMES, M.A.

All rights reserved.

HONEST SEX

*A Passionate Path to Deepen Connection
and Keep Relationships Alive*

ISBN

979-8-88504-630-5 *Paperback*

979-8-88504-948-1 *Kindle Ebook*

979-8-88504-835-4 *Digital Ebook*

I dedicate this book to the one in you who is able to pause until you can honestly communicate with vulnerability and care. It may not be easy, but I believe in you.

CONTENTS

Part 3   177

INTRODUCTION

———

"Really?" I said, looking toward the water bottle at the Target cash register that my husband was about to purchase en route to Burning Man. "Like we need more water bottles? Don't we have a dozen of them in our cupboards?"

"Mine leaks," he said. "You know how it goes in the desert. We can't mess around. I'm not going to go with a faulty water bottle. I remember when you got dehydrated in the desert, and it wasn't pretty."

"But it's plastic," I yelled, aware of the cashier warily eyeing us. "Think about the toxic island of plastic that is now the size of Texas and killing marine life," I said.

He glared at me. "We are about to have a life-changing experience," he shot back, "and this is what you want to focus on right now?"

"But we are not supposed to purchase corporate shit," I continued, unable to stop myself. "The point of this whole event is to reduce consumerism."

We went on like this, holding up the line at the checkout for a few more minutes before I gave in with a huff. This was a fight my husband and I had fifteen years ago, when we were still married. Burning Man, the festival that promotes self-expression, building temporary community, and anti-consumerism, required that we bring all of our food, shelter, and water. In the Black Rock desert, the elements were rough—dust and rain storms and extreme heat and cold. People pack for fun but also to survive.

Rather than trying to understand his point of view (which I can now see), I was so upset and overtaken by anxiety and my need to be right that I started an argument. Fights like these are one of the reasons our marriage ended a decade ago. And while the fights sometimes seemed to be about trivial matters, looking beyond the content reveals an immaturity in our communication that caused our relationship to break down.

You wouldn't think a fight about a water bottle would have anything to do with our sex life. However, a couple's sex life will not be intimate or exciting if they cannot share anxieties and desires in a way that creates closeness and understanding. There is no separating sex from the rest of a relationship, as hard as we try. If our communication does not bring us closer, it tears us apart. And as emotional connection diminishes, intimacy and sex usually do too.

My ex and I are not the only ones who fight over seemingly trivial things. The couples and singles I work with as a relationship coach bring similar everyday upsets and frustrations to our sessions. They do not always recognize that these surface conflicts are symptoms of deeper layers of hurt and fear. The deeper layers are more challenging to be honest about, both with others and ourselves.

Our fight was never about the water bottle.

My deeper layers included fears about values, money, and feeling misunderstood. I'm not the only one with these fears. It is common for people to focus on surface issues without seeing the deeper layers. Focusing on the surface layers means we are simultaneously hiding or avoiding our deeper pain. Both ways create disconnection, break trust, and can kill our sex lives.

Many of my clients have attempted to create intimacy and passion through methods akin to pruning flowers. Rather than focusing on trimming or trying to make flowers look beautiful—focusing on the surface aspects of life—we have to recognize that the soil is often missing necessary nutrients for the buds to grow—learning to be more honest and intimate in mature ways. Through coaching my clients, it became apparent that the soil—the foundation of relationships—needs to be healthier and stronger.

This means we need more than date nights and lingerie to keep passion alive and to bring it back when it fades. Better sex is not about new positions or toys. Although they can add fun and variety, they are not a replacement for honest connection. The fact that sex relies on much more than physicality is the missing link for many couples. We need to make fundamental shifts in our communication to keep relationships alive and exciting.

This book will give you the foundation for communication that creates more intimacy and makes sex more satisfying. This book is a guide for those who want to keep connection and passion alive in their relationships and for those who find romantic relationships more challenging than they imagined. It provides a path to the kind of intimacy people tell me they long for. In this book, I share the doorway I found back to connection and passion, which I do not see many people finding or opening. The doorway is a mature kind of honesty, and it is one of the most important nutrients in the soil needed for a couple to thrive. This book (*Honest Sex*) also explores aspects of sex that go beyond our limited cultural framework. This is the book I wish I was handed decades ago.

WE HAVE NOT MATURED ENOUGH TO SUSTAIN SATISFYING RELATIONSHIPS

Fifteen years after the water bottle argument, and ten years after our divorce, I was on a road trip with my ex and our kid. At the time, I was working on this book and reflecting on the lessons of the past decade. I told him I was sorry for the argument about the water bottle. I always tell my clients it is never too late to apologize or debrief a painful situation! I also apologized for all the times I was not mature enough to hear or validate his perspectives. He accepted my apology and we both expressed gratitude for how far we have come since we were married.

Mentioning our recent road trip to friends or acquaintances, I was often met with surprised responses like, "You're doing what with your ex-husband?" When he and I chose to move to a new state together, people were blown away. The fact that we respect each other and get along well enough to make major life changes together is a testament to the perspectives and tools shared in this book. We use them.

Although my marriage ended, I do not see this, or any couple's relationship ending, as a failure. Relationships can change form in healthy and positive ways, and at times, they come to a completion. Some people wonder if we are outgrowing marriage as a culture, but there is more to the relationship story than meets the eye. The problem I regularly see, and experienced in my marriage, is not that we have outgrown marriage or long-term relationships, but that we have actually not grown or matured enough to create the emotionally connected, sexually satisfying relationships we long for.

This book focuses on conscious communication and relating with examples of how these evolve into relationships that become more connected and passionate over time. The default romantic relationship stays on a surface level. Couples are not likely to consistently inquire into the deeper honesty of their partner's hearts and dreams. They shut down, rather than learn and grow through conflict. It takes courage and commitment to have a relationship with real connection and an intimate and exciting sex life, but the payoff is big!

Long-term relationships are struggling more and more these days. Marriage, for example, was in trouble long before I tried it fifteen years ago. Between 1960 and 1980, the divorce rate more than doubled—from 9.2 divorces per one thousand married women to 22.6 divorces per one thousand married women. The divorce rate hovers around 50 percent for first marriages and even higher for second and third ones.

The trend I see with clients, especially after a couple years of pandemic living, does not look good for marriage. Furthermore, those in long-term, unmarried relationships are also struggling to retain a hold on passion and commitment. (Wilcox, 2009)[1]

Couples are yearning to feel more bonded, supported, and attracted to each other. Over the past twenty years of coaching and facilitating workshops for thousands in the realms of communication and authenticity, it has become clear to me that turning the tide on relationships calls for a shift in relational dynamics.

WE CAN LEARN TO LOVE BETTER

This book was motivated by the fact that I do not want anyone to be humbled by a divorce or a breakup as I was. I thought I had relationships figured out! Looking back, I see that when I got married at age thirty, even after completing a master's in psychology, a decade of therapy, coaching, spiritual practice, yoga, tantric exploration, and self-growth workshops, I was still like a kindergartener who had not yet learned what it takes to keep love alive.

It has taken an incredible amount of additional humility and work on myself to unwind the relationship patterns I learned from a young age that broke love and connection, rather than supported it. My clients are courageously doing this too. They use the tools covered here to be honest and stay

---

1   According to the BBC online, during the pandemic, leading British law firm Stewarts logged a 122 percent increase in inquiries about divorce between July and October, compared with the same period last year.

true to themselves, while also respecting and communicating about others' needs. And even more than the wedding invites, housewarmings, and baby announcements I receive, what I love hearing from my clients is how they come to love and respect themselves.

I believe relationships can evolve, even when relational dynamics feel overwhelming or stuck. For this to happen, we need to learn a more mature and honest way of communicating. Mature honesty has the power to transform bickering, griping, nagging, irritation, and hurt into deep emotional connection and passionate sexual connection. It allows couples to get through fights about laundry and garbage, and even money and sex, to feel real and sustained closeness.

My hope is that my experiences will allow readers to identify pitfalls, rather than stumble into them. I hope to mitigate some of the frustration that occurs in relationships by revealing both my own and my clients' stories of vulnerability and learning to love better (names and personal details have been changed to respect clients' privacy). Learning these perspectives and tools could save *your* current and future relationships. They create the basis for honest relationships in which there is no need to hide who you really are and there is nothing you need to prove or live up to. You get to be you, wholly and honestly.

A NOTE ABOUT IDENTITY

I have explored and worked with people in a wide range of relationship models and do not believe that one relationship model fits all. I have witnessed relief when people find a relationship model that fits, rather than try to cover up dishonesty or inhabit a false self. Whether you are casually dating, in a traditional marriage, or in a throuple—you'll know what this is if it applies to you—you will find inspiration and tools to further your relationship goals.

As a cis-gendered, white woman who is mainly attracted to men, I know this book is biased by my perspective. I have found the principles in this book apply regardless of gender or biology, but most of my thousands of clients, while they come from many cultures around the world, have been in heterosexual relationships.

I also acknowledge that, even as a single mother and entrepreneur who has not always felt financially stable, I had the privilege of a financially secure, middle-class upbringing that set me up for a middle-class lifestyle as an adult. This has afforded me time and financial resources to explore relational dynamics. However, I do believe anyone can benefit from adopting a few of the honesty practices in this book, no matter how much time or money they have.

A GUIDE TO THE READER EXPERIENCE

This book is not designed to lean heavily into theory. My intent was to simplify concepts in a way that makes them actionable.

Part 1 of this book focuses on understanding what honesty is. It is much more complex than discerning whether someone is lying or telling the truth. Moving beyond this binary is a big leap in consciousness and becomes necessary to create relationships that grow and heal us.

Part 2 focuses on understanding what sex is. Sex is more expansive than I, or most of my clients, ever learned. Broadening our understanding opens up pathways of connection and passion that cannot exist otherwise.

Part 3 gives perspectives and tools that lead to stronger connection and intimacy, and thus more passion. You can use them immediately to strengthen your relationships.

You might be tempted to skip to the chapters on sex and orgasm, but understanding honesty is important, and most of us appreciate a little foreplay. Again, the foundation of better sex is not physical; it is emotional and relational. Part 1 lays the groundwork to improve not only your connections but your sex life as well.

Thousands of clients have expressed gratitude for the tools I share here that have allowed them to move beyond frustration and isolation to feel more energized, connected, and intimate in their relationships. I hope this book opens up new ways for you to love and be loved.

With love and honesty,
Shana

PART 1

CHAPTER 1

WHAT I WISH I LEARNED BEFORE I GOT MARRIED

———

My ten-year-old ran across the schoolyard as I finished a phone call with a friend going through a divorce. As I hung up, Ari said, "You look sad."

"I am sad," I said. "I was talking to Pueblo. He and Leah are getting divorced."

"What?" Ari asked incredulously. "Why is everyone getting divorced?" I paused to think about what to say.

"You know how you're learning to feel your emotions and find words to communicate respectfully, even when you're mad or sad?" I said. "And how you and I practice working things out together when we want different things, rather than stomping away or lashing out? Most of us parents did not learn how to do this skillfully when we were young. That makes marriage really hard. Thankfully, your generation is learning how."

In witnessing my friends' and clients' relationships, I saw dynamics similar to my own. We all struggled with immature and ineffective communication and relational strategies. If we had been equipped to navigate these differences consciously, our relationships might have weathered the storms and become stronger as a result. We could have learned to keep connection and intimacy healthy and satisfying.

THE CURRENT RELATIONSHIP CRISIS

As a divorced person in my forties, I see that much of the suffering I have experienced in relationships could have been prevented if I had grown up with a social-emotional education about romantic relationships. Instead, what I experienced in my sex education classes was very clinical and biological—focused on things like fallopian tubes, tampons, and how to put a condom on a banana. As it stands, I have now been in romantic relationships with a variety of people in four decades of my life. I have gleaned information about why my and many others' relationships break down. I believe we are in the midst of a relationship crisis where the current default toolset is not powerful enough to withstand the inevitable challenges of relationships. Yet there are tools we can use from a variety of self-growth, psychological, and spiritual modalities.

The education system in the 1980s and '90s did not teach much useful information about relationships or sex when I was growing up, as evidenced by the condom on the banana episode. The instructional policy at the time varied by district across the United States. Some areas advised puberty-age students to practice abstinence only. Others taught only medically accurate information about the reproductive system with an emphasis on birth control. Neither approach looked realistically at human sexual behavior. Teens are naturally curious about sex. Some will have sex, and others will at least want to explore relationships with romantic partners.

To support a realistic view of human sexuality, we could have been taught age-appropriate, healthy foundations of communication, emotional intelligence, and connection. We could have learned how our minds, emotions, and bodies work, both on our own and in relation to others'. Instead, my eighth grade "sex-ed" class was mainly about anatomy. Our teacher's Friday wisdom was "Have a good weekend and keep your pants on." This is far from what the World Health Organization proposes as a definition of sexual health:

"Sexual health is the integration of the somatic, emotional, intellectual, and social aspects of sexual being, in ways that are positively enriching and that enhance personality, communication, and love. Fundamental to this concept are the right to sexual information and the right to pleasure." (Planned Parenthood 2022)

With a vacuum of information about humanity and sexuality, my compass sadly became peer pressure and magazines. My actions were arranged to stave off others' judgments, which was tricky because I was just as afraid of being called a prude as I was of being called a slut. Looking back, I wish I had heard the word sacred in relation to my body, relationships, and sexuality, like I finally heard in communication and sensuality trainings in my twenties. I'll discuss more about this in Chapter 5. I wish I was encouraged to value what I liked, more than what made me likable. Learning relationship basics from *Cosmopolitan* magazine and friends made relationships possible, but it takes much more than that for relationships to survive and even more to thrive.

Much of the math, science, and history I learned in school, I no longer use. After leaving school, I constantly continue to relate to and collaborate with others. I create and maintain relationships with family, friends, and romantic and business partners. Unfortunately, I had to piece together an education for myself about human relationships. It is no wonder I have rarely found a conscious romantic relationship upon which to model mine.

SELF-AWARENESS IS A FOUNDATION OF LASTING, THRIVING RELATIONSHIPS

Alain de Botton, a British philosopher and author, writes about what I see as a crisis in his *New York Times* article, "Why You Will Marry the Wrong Person." "Marriage," he writes, "ends up as a hopeful, generous, infinitely kind gamble taken by two people who don't know yet who they are or who the other might be, binding themselves to a future they cannot conceive of and have carefully avoided investigating." This quote struck a nerve with me because I had never heard someone illuminate this dynamic so clearly and succinctly. (de Botton, 2016)

With our lack of human and relational education, marriage and long-term relationships are more of a gamble than many people realize. Clients often come to me as they are evolving into a new version of themselves. The new version does not always fit into the romantic relationship they committed to years or decades before, especially if their partner is not growing.

It may be that the painful journey de Botton writes about is part of our human condition, the sand in an oyster that forces us to mature and love better. Through rubbing up against the painful, confronting aspects of our relationships, we can eventually emerge with a pearl—the capacity to relate in a truly loving and mature way. But I often wish I received a manual when I was young. De Botton writes "before marriage we rarely delve into our complexities." He hits the nail on the head with the importance of self-awareness. Relationships become smoother and kinder the more self-aware we become. The more aware we are of the habits and past wounding that cause recurring upsets, the better chance we have of remaining connected through chaos and conflict. These days, people are getting married later, so there is a better chance of being more self-aware, but it takes a long time—some would say a lifetime—to consciously navigate the wounding we all have from childhood and subsequent relationships.

Though we will inevitably disagree or be upset with a partner at times, an increasing willingness to vulnerably share our self-awareness will make us more connected. Likewise, the better able we are to receive our partners' differences with curiosity and compassion, the closer we will feel. I would like to change the trajectory of de Botton's prediction, "when relationships threaten to reveal our flaws, we blame our partners and call it a day." Instead of bailing on relationships, we can learn to deepen connection and intimacy. We can use the conflicts and upsets that tear most couples apart to build more powerful and loving bonds.

But aren't optimal relationships supposed to be conflict-free? I hear this question from clients frequently.

Though I wish it were not true, I see conflict and upsets as inevitable in relationships. Drs. John and Julie Gottman direct a Love Lab that has done innovative research into the dynamics of thousands of couples' romantic relationships. They found it was not conflict that killed a couple's chance of staying together; rather, what indicated future failure was *how* they treated each other in the midst of conflict. (Gottman, 2006)

The Gottmans found that couples whose dynamic involved criticism, contempt, defensiveness, and stonewalling—termed "the Four Horsemen of the Apocalypse"—were much more likely to break up or get divorced. What determined the success of a relationship was how much each partner could show up with self-awareness and minimize the presence of the Four Horsemen. So it is not the simple presence of conflict that sends relationships over the rocky ledge; it is how we deal with conflict. I've found that a surface approach to conflict rarely works.

WE NEED TO LOOK DEEPER THAN THE SURFACE CONFLICT

I watched as my mom picked up the phone and exclaimed, "Twenty more minutes? You said you'd be home fifteen minutes ago!" She rolled her eyes as she hung up and sighed. Dinner was warm, and we were both sitting at the table, hungry.

Through the phone I heard my dad say, "My meeting went later than I expected. I can't just walk out on a client. What do you expect me to do?"

As a little girl, I watched my parents fight about being on time. I sat at the kitchen table while my dad attempted to calm my mom down. On the surface, my mom was upset because my dad was late. On the surface, my dad was annoyed about being managed. But this is clearly not the whole story. They both felt unappreciated. They both had needs that were not being met, but they did not know how to say so.

I remember sitting there, not yet a teenager, knowing this conflict went much deeper than being on time. I realized there were more layers in their interactions than they, or I, were aware of. The topics they argued about are what I call the surface layer. Most couples have to navigate these—chores, bills, laundry, money, and so on. These topics are more apparent than the underlying layers, so they are an easier target to pick a fight about.

Hiding beneath the surface though, are more complex and vulnerable layers that can remain unseen, unaddressed, and unresolved. These layers include upsets and disappointments that stem from the tension and pain of being unsupported, unsafe, or misunderstood. These layers also hold the vulnerable parts we carry around with us from childhood experiences of loss and pain.

When *I* got frustrated with an ex who was late, it appeared I was upset about his time management, but that was a surface layer. Deep down, I was wondering whether he respected and prioritized me. Maybe my mom also had these thoughts about my dad. And because our feelings are heightened by experiences from our history, the stress around time management from my childhood exacerbated my reactions to him.

The underlying layers are much more effective and impactful to talk about than the surface layers. They are also what needs to be addressed for conflict to actually resolve. But, since many people are not aware they exist under the surface, they remain unaddressed. This creates a dynamic where repeated conversations do not access the deeper layers that can heal the pain and reconnect.

As I work with singles and couples in their relationship struggles, I see what keeps us hovering at surface levels, rather than revealing the deeper layers. First, the fear of rejection is so powerful—even when unconscious—that by comparison, painful, recurring dynamics seem like a better option. Second, many people I work with say they do not know how to communicate in a way that creates connection and intimacy, especially in the midst of upsetting and painful experiences.

When we do not learn how to honestly communicate our fears and feelings, we are more likely to explode or distance ourselves when we feel hurt or upset. Similarly, when our fear of rejection runs the show, we are less likely to slow down, self-reflect, and consciously communicate.

I remember a moment with an ex when he told me he did not want to live with kids again. He had already raised two kids who were in college and was in a different stage of life. He was ready to focus more on himself. We had been dating long enough that hearing that felt like a blow. I wanted a partner who would create a blended family with me. I felt a flash of anger as I felt alone, even abandoned. Tension rippled through my body. It felt like my chest was full of barbed wire. Heat rose to my face. I felt like an animal about to pounce.

I almost screamed at him, but instead I breathed deeply and practiced getting in touch with my more vulnerable parts. I felt the sadness and loneliness I sometimes experience as I parent my child alone. I managed not to lash out or call him selfish. Nor did I store my upset to use as ammunition for a later time. Instead, I found the words, "I need a minute. I am going to be silent so I don't say something I'll regret. I'm going to close my eyes until I can say something that will create more connection, rather than less." Instead of a fight, we had a conscious conversation about our needs and fears. Afterward, we felt closer, rather than distant or angry. Even though we recognized differences in our desires, we kept our hearts open and our words respectful.

Most of us were never taught an alternative to exploding or distancing. We can hesitate to share our fears because we might be seen as unlovable or even worse, be abandoned. When the risk of revealing ourselves seems too great, we can even reject ourselves before we can be rejected by another. Hiding our truth and lashing out with judgments are two common ways we do this.

Just as air fuels fire, honesty fuels connection and passion. Likewise, fires extinguish without air, and passion and intimacy extinguish without honesty. Throughout this book, I give tools to support the kind of honesty that creates connection, rather than the kind that sends people running for the hills. For now, let's look at an example of what happened to a client who avoided honesty.

IT'S NOT ABOUT THE TEA, THE GARBAGE, OR ANY SURFACE CONTENT

My client, Lisa, relayed this story to me in one of our sessions. She said . . .

I was walking down the stairs with a load of laundry in one hand and a raw chicken in the other. My house was in total shambles because we had just moved. The refrigerator wasn't even in the kitchen.

I was rushing around, trying to balance the laundry with the chicken and pick up my kid's clothes that were all over the floor when my husband passed me on the stairs. He asked me to make him some tea.

I nodded, agreeing outwardly, but inside I was infuriated! Couldn't he see I was doing three things already? It was exasperating. I wanted him to do it himself. But I didn't say that. Instead, I dumped the laundry in the washer, turned on the kettle for hot water, and started making my kid breakfast.

I was cracking eggs and had just dropped a juice cup on the floor when my husband came into the kitchen and frowned. I immediately felt defensive and asked why he was looking at me like that. "I asked you to make tea," he said. "You said you would and you didn't."

At that point I lost it. "You can't be serious!" I screamed.

The tea bag was in the mug and the kettle was steaming. How the *fuck* could he be upset with me? Why couldn't he pour the damn water over the tea bag himself while I was taking care of *everything* else he and our kid needed? Why does he need me to do everything?

I yelled, "Make your own damn tea and leave me alone." I couldn't help myself!

As Lisa and I talked, we rewound and slowed down the situation to see why she exploded and how she could have gotten more of what she wanted. We both knew it was not about the tea. That was just the surface content. She thought back to walking down the stairs, laundry and chicken in hand, and realized what she really wanted was help. If she had been honest in that moment, she would have said something like, "I have my hands full. Could you please take the laundry or the chicken? And can you make your tea while I make our kid's breakfast?"

Why wasn't she honest? Why, instead of asking for what she wanted, did she agree to make his tea?

I often see that people have desires for help, connection, touch, understanding, and listening that are not met in their relationships. Sometimes it is because they are never asked for.

As we talked, we saw that Lisa had an old belief that women are not supposed to need help. She was supposed to do it all— her career, housework, childcare—without complaint. This would make her a "good wife." She had developed a habit of automatically saying *yes* when people asked her to do things, even if she did not want to because she felt she would end up alone and angry if she didn't. While he of course played his part, the lack of honesty on her part created disconnection with her husband in all areas of life, including her sex life.

LACK OF HONESTY OUTSIDE THE BEDROOM
IMPACTS WHAT HAPPENS INSIDE THE BEDROOM

Lisa tells me she is not being honest in her sex life either. She does not speak up when sex does not feel good. When her husband touches her in a way that is uncomfortable, she does not want to hurt his feelings by saying so. This may seem hard to believe for a powerful, professional woman, but I can relate. I have not always spoken up, and I have worked with hundreds of women—and people of all genders—who do not either. It is common for people to worry about what will happen if they are honest, especially in the bedroom.

It is no surprise that Lisa does not enjoy sex with her husband anymore. She imagines her sexual fulfillment has become a lost cause, forecasting that she will never be touched or under-stood in a way she wants to be. Being honest and asking for what she wants seems like hard work with very little chance of a payoff. Many of my clients reflect that it seems easier to remain in an unsatisfied state, in which they have some control in their relationship, rather than risk being rejected.

This is known as preferring the "certainty of misery rather than the misery of uncertainty." We all do this at some point in our lives because being honest feels extremely vulnerable. In the underlying layers, we find fear and tenderness. For instance, Lisa worries: What if what I want is not what he wants, would our relationship have to end? What if he gets mad at me? What if there is something about me that he doesn't like or finds displeasing?

Lisa found the courage to have honest conversations with her husband. Although they did not resolve all of their differences, she solved a bigger issue. Lisa recovered parts of herself she had let go of long ago. She recovered her strength, clarity, and a capacity to honestly speak up for herself.

Communicating our honesty is not easy, especially when we have not done so for years, but my clients and I have found it is worth the risk. By doing so, we get more of what we want, both in and out of the bedroom. We experience more vitality and connection, rather than dullness and disconnection. And whether the relationship stays together or not, there is respect and peace, rather than hostility and resentment. Honesty also helps us determine sooner, rather than later, whether we are a good match. We then do not have to waste our precious time and energy.

The problems Lisa and my mom dealt with illustrate different ends of the spectrum of outward expression that occur when honesty is avoided. Some people yell. Some people shut down. But underneath, they feel angry and hopeless, unheard, and unfulfilled. I find this heartbreaking.

Being honest when something does not feel good allows us to avoid creating baggage that kills connection and passion. I was reminded of this when I spent a day bleeding as I cut back dead, spiky blackberry vines out of my garden. I cursed every time I got poked with a thorn, realizing that if I had done this months before, I would not be bloody. The longer we wait to tell the truth, the messier and "bloodier" it gets.

From the example of my parents' fight about time, more mature honesty reveals that my mom may have felt overwhelmed, misunderstood, or alone, but that is not what she communicated.

My dad may have felt attacked or unappreciated, but that is not what he said. If we do not learn to discuss the deeper issues and communicate our actual needs and desires, relationships remain fraught with painful, recurring conflict.

The couples who come to me communicating in bitter, combative, or tense ways do not feel connected. They are not having much sex, and if they are having sex at all, it is not the kind that is nourishing, satisfying, or ecstatic. Intimacy and sex will rarely be good, and never exceptional, without mature honesty. But it is easy to remain strangers to our partners when our fear of rejection is stronger than the pain of remaining unfulfilled. In being honest, we take a risk, but we already know what happens when we hide our truth and hope things will change. When we learn to communicate more honestly, we give intimacy a chance to flourish.

PRACTICE

To learn to be honest in a more mature way, we have to start to pay attention to our reactions and responses, separating the surface layer from the deeper layers.

When I support clients to get in touch with the deeper layers and create more genuine connections with others, we talk about how we begin to "see the water we are swimming in." In other words, we shift from being like a fish, unaware of its watery surroundings, to being conscious of our habits, choices, and the impacts we have on others. As we become aware of what we were previously unconscious of, we gain choice about what we say and do.

On a date years ago, I was talking about my life and business to an insightful man. He was a chiropractor with an easygoing manner and a sparkle in his eyes. At one point, he paused and said, "I am focused on similar things in my life, but for you, they sound urgent."

The word "urgent" echoed in my ears, as I could suddenly see that most of my experiences were being filtered through the lens of anxious *urgency*. This was the water I was swimming in, which I had not previously seen. I wanted everything I created in my life and business to happen *now* and was worried time was running out. Even though we only went on a few dates, this clarity has guided me for years, even in the midst of publishing this book.

When we are not conscious of our habits, fears, hurts, and vulnerabilities, we can unintentionally hurt ourselves and our partners. Once we become aware of our default habits and reactions, we have the ability to choose our behaviors and move toward connection.

To honestly communicate, we have to become aware of these deeper layers. To gain self-awareness, we will focus on developing what many spiritual teachers call the Witness Consciousness. Start by making a list of three to five situations where you felt upset with someone in your life. You can keep this for your eyes only if you are worried about how others will respond.

Use this sentence stem to write the emotions you feel with each situation:

I feel [insert feeling word: angry, irritated, annoyed, upset, etc.] that [insert situation].

When you write about the situation, write what happened in as concrete a way as possible. Being concrete means to think about an experience objectively. For example, the phrase "leaving dishes in the sink" is more concrete than "being messy," which is vague and carries a negative judgment. Pointing out that someone "rolled their eyes" is more concrete than saying they "seemed irritated," which they could also argue they were not. Write your situation with objective specifics that are as inarguable as possible. If your partner "said nothing when you asked a question," that is inarguable. Calling your partner "selfish" is your opinion, and thus is arguable.

Some examples are:

- *I feel angry that I emptied the dishwasher every time we ran it last week.*

- *I feel upset that [Name] was late yesterday.*

- *I felt explosive when [Name] said, "You did that wrong."*

I feel [_____] that [_____].

I feel [_____] that [_____].

I feel [_____] that [_____].

I feel [_____] that [_____].

I feel [_____] that [_____].

This is the beginning of creating more effective communication with a partner, but do not worry about taking action yet. We will get there later in this book. For now, simply complete your sentence stems with three to five situations.

Next, we'll look at a deeper layer so you can start to see the layers beneath the garbage, laundry, and other surface content that upsets you. These will eventually allow you to connect with your partners on a deeper level. Ask yourself: What is important about this situation that upsets me? Do your best to stay away from right and wrong or regarding one person's way as better than another's. Focus on clarifying what matters to you. By writing this down, you will be prepared the next time the issue arises. This step will give you clarity about how to talk about it with honesty and compassion.

Here's an example from my life:

I want the kitchen sink clean at the end of each day. This has created conflicts with partners who have a different cleanup style. When I have communicated about this, it went much better when I shared the deeper layers and why this preference is important to me.

For me, getting myself ready for work and my kid ready for school in the morning is stressful. It is important to me that it is as smooth as possible. When the sink is cluttered, I feel overwhelmed. It takes time and attention away from the other tasks I need to accomplish. I want the morning to go as smoothly as possible so everyone starts their day with as much positive feeling as we can have.

This is more inspiring for a partner to hear than a complaint about dirty dishes!

Your turn:

_____

_____

_____

_____

_____

_____

_____

One more aspect of communication that creates more connection is to discover what makes us feel vulnerable about sharing our truth. Try filling in this sentence stem with at least one situation:

What feels vulnerable about this for me is . . .

A cluttered kitchen sink feels vulnerable because (similar to Lisa) I'm worried my partner won't want to be with me if I don't do all the cleaning myself. I know this is an outdated gender role, but I genuinely have this fear and worry my partner will be upset with me if I ask him to help. I want to bring more joy and vitality to my romantic relationship, and I am more likely to do this when we work together to keep our environment organized, but I'm afraid to ask.

What feels vulnerable about the upsets you wrote down?

_____

_____

_____

_____

_____

_____

_____

Everything you find here will be a doorway to connect deeply with yourself and those you love. By doing the exercises in this book and reflecting on both what goes well and what needs work, you become the more objective, loving presence for yourself that it takes to strengthen your relationship.

This may not be easy to do on your own. At times, help from a friend will be enough. At other times, working with a professional coach or therapist will help alleviate unnecessary suffering. There is no shame in getting support. I have had dozens of therapists, coaches, and guides along the way, and I still turn to them for help. If you feel depressed, overwhelmed, stuck, or are struggling with your mental health, please seek professional guidance. Take your time and be gentle with yourself as you explore. Everyone I know struggles with relationship dynamics in one way or another. You are not alone!

CHAPTER 2

WHAT IS HONESTY AND HOW CAN WE CULTIVATE MATURE HONESTY?

———

The fear that my honesty would destroy a relationship has caused conflicts in the past. One time I was lying in bed with a boyfriend, eager to have an important conversation. I spent a week trying to find a good time for it because we had so little time together. We were next to each other; his eyes were closed as I looked at him. I really wanted to talk, but I told myself he was too tired and went to sleep without initiating the conversation.

The next morning I was grumpy. When he asked why I was not as upbeat as usual, I admitted I wanted to talk about something last night, but I didn't bring it up because he looked tired, and now I was disappointed.

"Why didn't you ask me to have the conversation?" he asked.

"Because you looked exhausted," I said, hoping he would feel cared for.

"I was tired, but if it mattered to you, I would have talked about it," he said, frustrated that I was upset with him for a decision I made for him.

Thanks to my conditioned habits, I withheld my honesty to try to take care of the needs I imagined he had. They were not his actual needs. I feared he would get upset and maybe even want to end our relationship (I know it may sound crazy, but our fears can be that strong!). In the end, he was upset with me anyway, and I did not tell him what I needed to feel more connected with him.

Honesty is one of the bedrocks of romantic relationships. I think most people would agree that relationships break down when we are not honest. But that does not make it easy to say what we are afraid to say. A lack of honesty between people makes it difficult to relax, trust, and feel safe. When we don't feel safe, we are likely to close our minds, hearts, and bodies. Where love once flowed freely, walls go up, distance grows, generosity wanes, and we become colder or more bitter toward our partners. A healthy, intimate sex life also falls to the wayside when this happens.

Those who do not see themselves as dishonest may be tempted to skip this chapter. Why would we need a better understanding of honesty when we are already being honest? How could honesty be a new way to reignite and sustain passion and intimacy when we are already doing it?

In many relationships, however, I noticed honesty is missing key elements, which leads unknowingly to relationship struggles. There is a lot more to honesty than most people recognize! This is not an individual failing but a widespread cultural trend causing hardship in relationships.

CONVENTIONAL HONESTY NEEDS AN UPGRADE

Christian Miller, philosopher and author of Honesty: The Philosophy and Psychology of a Neglected Virtue, reveals there are only two articles about honesty published in the past fifty years in the field of philosophy (aside from the work his team published). "Sadly," he writes, "honesty has gone missing in recent decades. It is largely absent from academic research. It seems to be rare in society. And it is not commonly found in discussions of how to become a better person."

With the public discussion about honesty on the back burner for decades, our current operating definition and sense of honesty are not very nuanced or evolved. When we take a more philosophical look at honesty, as Miller suggests, we see the conventional expression of honesty – not lying – is only a small part of it. Miller points out that honesty is also counter to actions like cheating, bullshitting, hypocrisy, and promise-breaking. He also adds self-deception, which I believe is one of the key habits we must overcome to evolve and mature our honesty.

In this chapter, I distinguish conventional honesty from what I call "mature honesty." Beyond the simple binary of lying or truth-telling, mature honesty involves a commitment to respect, compassion, and personal responsibility. It calls on the grown-up, evolved aspects of our psyches and souls to take the lead. It demands we look beneath our surface reactions to discover the real, vulnerable reasons we get upset.

HOW CONVENTIONAL HONESTY DESTROYS RELATIONSHIPS

Many of us have a misguided understanding of honesty that inadvertently allows us to tap into a host of negative emotions and communication styles, including blame, shame, name-calling, and attacking. At times, we accuse, judge, or "say it like it is" to others, telling an incomplete story from a one-sided perspective. It may sound like this:

"I was not being an asshole...YOU were being a jerk."

"I am not unreasonable...YOU are maddening."

Receivers likely defend themselves or attack back, often using a combative tone and heaping on the blame, focusing on who did what or who let down. Someone, at some point, often exclaims: "What? I'm just being honest!" This creates a downward spiral that breaks trust and kills attraction. This type of honesty does not take any responsibility for the hurtful tone or the harmful blaming and shaming. This book intends to show you other options for this immature type of honesty so you can break the cycle of destructive interactions.

We must first recognize what has been termed "life-alienating communication" by Marshall Rosenberg, a clinical psychologist and founder of the Nonviolent Communication (NVC) process. Rosenberg refers to "any form of communication that blocks our ability to focus on our core humanity and establish real connections." He listed moralistic judgments, name-calling, comparisons, denial of responsibility, and demands (as opposed to requests) as life-alienating or violent types of communication. Saying "you're a jerk" or "you're maddening" to someone is making a moralistic judgment and name-calling. It provokes more of the same and does not strengthen the connection. (Rosenburg, 2022)

Until we recognize that this superficial form of honesty is actually doing violence to our relationships, we will unknowingly blame, shame, and use irresponsible and life-alienating language against those we love. True honesty comes from a more mature place in our psyche and focuses on becoming more conscious of our feelings about and reactions to others. It takes full responsibility for these feelings and reactions rather than shifting blame onto the other.

These peaceful alternatives to the violent communication many of us grew up with are helpful and healing for relationship dynamics. In the 1980s, Rosenberg, who grew up in a turbulent Detroit neighborhood, started the Center for Nonviolent Communication and began teaching people to create more harmony in all social relationship dynamics, from romantic couples to nations in conflict. NVC has since grown into a world-renowned communication process.

NVC reveals how our words, even those that seem conventionally honest, can create painful dynamics, often unintentionally. In contrast, Rosenberg describes the basics of NVC as "expressing ourselves with clarity, compassion, self-responsibility, empathy, and the common good in mind." The NVC process guides people to share objective observations and feelings, needs, and requests. This is counter to expressing our judgments through blaming, shaming, or name-calling, which is likely to put others on the defense.

In the above interaction, instead of calling the other person a jerk, the first speaker would have spoken to the other person's behavior as objectively as possible and expressed their feeling of frustration about the impact. "I felt frustrated when you didn't acknowledge how I was trying to help you," they might have said. Then, they could make a request, "Will you acknowledge my helpful behaviors when you notice them?" This moves the conversation towards connection and rehabilitates their communication. We'll look at more ways to use the methods of NVC soon. But first, it's helpful to understand why we so easily fall into the default mode of destructive interactions.

WHY IS CONVENTIONAL HONESTY SO COMMON?

Susan Campbell is a renowned therapist and the author of Getting Real and Five Minute Relationship Repair. She has been one of the foremost teachers of honesty for nearly fifty years. She agrees that honesty is more complicated than it first seems and that many people do not know how to communicate honestly in a mature or conscious way.

In a conversation with Campbell, she mentioned honesty as "the ability to know and reveal what you're feeling, thinking and wanting." While this sounds simple, she acknowledges the self-awareness this demands is anything but easy. To know what we feel and think, we first have to understand what she calls our "conditioned habits of feeling and thinking, that we will probably keep discovering until the day we die, especially if we stay in relationships."

According to Merriam-Webster, honest means "sincere, free of deceit, and untruthfulness." This definition is based on our ability to know ourselves. Unfortunately, humans can think we know ourselves while we unconsciously deceive ourselves. It is common for our deeper fears, needs, and motivations to remain unconscious. When I initially ask clients what they feel or want, they often respond, "I don't know." As we explore, insights and clarity arise that they never were previously aware of. We cannot be honest with ourselves or our partners about what remains in our subconscious.

Our history and life experience form conditioned views that shape how we perceive and react to different situations. For example, one person may feel offended by being called good-looking, while another may feel flattered. The first person may have received negative or unsafe attention for their looks throughout life, while the second may have felt celebrated. I remind my clients that conditioned habits form as we grow up, often unbeknownst to us, to combat the shame they feel about their limited or distorted views.

When behaviors are deemed respectable and lovable to our caretakers, peers, and communities, we are conditioned to do more of them. When behaviors are considered bad or unlovable, we often do less of them. In simple terms, if our caretakers give us attention and praise for being considerate, we are likely to create an identity that upholds this.

We may prioritize being considerate over being genuine or honest, thinking we must always consider others' needs first for people to like, love, or want to be with us. Saying "yes" to people's requests when we would rather say "no" is part of prioritizing being nice over being honest.

I will never forget the night about ten years ago when a colleague asked me to cover for him for a relationship workshop we both facilitated. I said "no" because I was choosing to prioritize self-care that weekend. But when we hung up the phone, I was terrified he would never respect or trust me again. I cried for hours, facing the old thoughts and feelings engrained from this conditioned belief that formed at a young age.

That night, I reflected on the love and praise I received for being the peacemaker in my family when I was growing up. I tried to help everyone get along and solidified a pattern of sacrificing my desires to keep the peace. Now it is sometimes challenging to know whether I am excited by a partner's desire or whether I want something different. I have to cut through fog and confusion, the "disappearing" of my desires, and the fear that my honesty could destroy our relationship. I have to take time, often through journaling, meditation, or self-reflection, to figure out what is true for me. If I don't, I eventually become resentful or dissatisfied. This happens with my clients whose desires remain unconscious or unspoken, too.

"To the extent you are aware of conditioned habits of thinking and feeling, you'll be able to be more honest," Campbell says. Gaining awareness of these conditioned habits is the first step. As Rosenberg taught in the NVC process, we do this by learning to pay attention to our objective observations and expressing needs and requests rather than judgments.

CONVENTIONAL HONESTY IN ACTION

Our friends were moving house, and I was not planning to help pack their truck. One morning, as we discussed this, my ex told me I was being selfish and uncaring. We were sitting in the living room when he said this to me, and I remember feeling so offended that I felt like leaping off the couch to strangle him. (I did not.)

"WHAT?" I yelled. "You can't be serious! I am not caring enough??"

Me? I thought. The one who constantly tries to take care of everyone around me, going out of my way to make sure people feel included, cared for, and supported. This was NOT debatable to the part of me that was conditioned to identify as a CARING person. I often felt guilt and shame when I said "no' to people's requests. Saying "no" to our friends was not easy for me, and when he judged me for it, a hot rage surged inside me. I was compelled to defend my image.

With mature honesty, we respond in curious rather than defensive ways. Neither one of us did a great job in this situation. Let's look at how each side of the communication went and where we veered into immaturity.

On my side, I could have revealed the underlying vulnerability and pain rather than attacking with my hurt, angry tone. I could have said something like, "Ouch. I think I am constantly trying really hard to take care of others, so it is confusing and painful that you see me as selfish."

My ex focused on the surface-level content – his judgments about me. This is a sign of immature honesty. Mature honesty is communicated from a deeper place than our initial defenses or critiques and involves personal vulnerability.

Instead of saying I was selfish or uncaring, he could have revealed his vulnerability by saying something like, "When you said no to helping our friends, I felt afraid of their judgment and of being seen as selfish." Or he could have said, "I notice I feel sad because I want us to help our friends together, both to be helpful and to be with you. I feel disappointed to go alone." These statements reveal his internal thoughts and feelings rather than his external judgments about me.

One of the cornerstones of immature honesty is that we often try to be right and make someone else wrong. But when a partner reveals personal vulnerability, the other feels less compelled to defend themselves. Had we each revealed our vulnerability, the conversation would have led to us knowing and supporting each other. Instead, it wedged us farther apart. If we do not evolve to communicate our honesty from a deeper place, beyond the surface hurts and upsets, fights go in one of two unhelpful directions — a battle of character attacks and defensiveness or a retreat into a state of defeat and hopelessness. Both break trust and respect. Finding the deeper, more vulnerable content brings hope for reconnection and reigniting passion.

We can start to notice our conditioned habits by recognizing that they often come with feelings of upset, agitation, disconnection, or even numbness. As we become aware of this and begin to check in with our states of mind, we can break our unconscious habits. Instead of lashing out or pulling away, for example, we can practice coming closer by revealing our honest feelings at the moment. Some powerful statements we can make to a partner that counteract our negative habits are: "I was about to pull away," "I can feel the part of me that wants to lash out," or "For some reason, I am really agitated right now." Sharing like this allows us to stay connected, even amid an upset. This is honesty in its mature form.

Let's look more at how we can access our vulnerability and simultaneously help others become curious and compassionate when we express our pain. This mature and effective honesty creates a foundation for connection and passion for thriving in relationships.

FACETS OF MATURE HONESTY

Mature honesty and Rosenberg's NVC share the goal of a more humane way of communicating that fosters connection and intimacy. While I was never formally trained in NVC, its influence has filtered into so many areas of self-development that I feel indebted to its perspectives and process.

The fastest path I teach for clients to access mature honesty is the willingness to get more vulnerable. Vulnerability turns our attention from attack or blame to a responsible, compassionate view. Many of us avoid this because it feels scarier to take down our walls than it does to attack. As we become aware of our wounds and habits that cause us to react in disrespectful ways, and as we get vulnerable and let go of life-alienating language, we have the capacity to choose mature honesty more often.

To access this vulnerability and get honest from a deeper place, we can first check to see whether what we want to say includes blaming or accusatory statements. If so, we look for an objective observation instead. Instead of saying "You were mean," which is not vulnerable, we could say, "My feelings were hurt." We can also add the impact we felt as a result. For example, "You were rude when you ignored my project and talked about yourself," becomes "I felt sad when I told you about my project, and you changed the subject without asking a question."

Shifting our language makes it less likely that someone will want to defend themselves. It also makes it more likely we will get our needs met. Telling someone they are being mean is less likely to elicit compassion than when we tell them our feelings were hurt. We can take this one step further by acknowledging our past wounds. For example, "In my family, I often felt talked over and unseen. I likely felt more upset because of that."

To evoke mature honesty, we can ask ourselves questions like: "What feels vulnerable to me about this?" or "What am I struggling with beyond my initial reaction?" These questions help us go deeper into our own experiences rather than blame someone else. We can ask ourselves, "How can I express my struggle with my partner's behavior without making them wrong?" We can also ask ourselves, "What would I need to feel connected again?" A well-known question from NVC is, "What are my/their unmet needs right now?" These questions allow us to access a mature kind of honesty where we can collaborate and make requests rather than punish others or give up on our needs.

MATURE HONESTY IN CONVERSATION

Years ago, my partner and I had a conversation that epitomized how mature honesty can upgrade a relationship. We both shared that, despite our great chemistry, we were not as attracted to each other as we had been to others. We wondered together whether this was a deal-breaker.

For many people, this conversation would have been a nightmare. Tempers could have flared, and accusations could have flown, as feelings of hurt and hopelessness decreased our self-esteem. But, because we committed to the mature honesty this chapter lays out, we stayed connected through a very tender topic. While hearing his truth was difficult, I practiced remaining curious. I accessed a part of me that was more mature than my surface consciousness, simmering with hurt and anger and wanting to escape from fear. The deeper and more secure part of me wanted to hear his honesty and discover my own, even if it meant a major change in our relationship.

A sign of immature honesty is that it instigates arguments that create pain and break trust. Mature honesty strengthens intimacy by revealing deeper, more vulnerable truths. Through supporting hundreds of conversations, I have seen this evoke aliveness (even when they are uncomfortable to hear). Continuing with the topic of attraction, for example, when we hide our waning attraction for a partner, it is common to feel numb or separate. As we try to avoid the discomfort of acknowledging fizzling attraction, we inevitably shut down. Numbness and distance both kill attraction, even when unintentional. When we are honest in a mature and connected way, we can discover new possibilities together. With attraction and other topics that can be scary to address, we can explore subtleties to see whether other factors have been at play, like hormonal changes, a break in trust, a disappointment that got swept under the rug, or some other instigating event. My partner and I may have realized we were not a romantic fit in our conversation about chemistry vs. attraction. If that happened, I would rather have set each other free than continue to drain our precious life energy pretending or trying to make it work. As it happened, we felt closer and more turned on to each other.

I know it can be more intimidating to have these conversations within a marriage or a long-term relationship because it is easy to fear the worst outcome – separation. But when we face what is real, even when painful, we access our sovereignty and creativity. We find ways to be connected that we could not have imagined previously. When my clients reconnect emotionally with a partner, I see romantic attraction return. This has proved to me that attraction goes far beyond physicality, and honesty is one of its foundations.

It reminds me of the quote by Elizabeth Apell, "And the day came when the risk to remain tight in a bud was more painful than the risk it took to blossom." Getting honest is a risk, but hiding or ignoring parts of ourselves often becomes more painful. It may not be easy to share honesty maturely, but it can create a more powerful bond and reignite attraction. The shift from immature to mature honesty opens up new dimensions of freedom and love that couples do not access when hiding their authentic selves. (Apell, 1979)

Campbell says we will discover more about ourselves and peel away the layers of false identities and conditioning until our dying day because of how complex and multilayered honesty is. "At almost 80 years old," she told me, "I am still discovering my unconscious motivations."

MATURE HONESTY INCLUDES SELF-REVEALING

It is never easy to tell someone that, for example, you do not like the way they touch you, that how they deal with money makes you feel hopeless about a future together, or that you need more help. It is not easy to bring up these topics at all, let alone consciously, in a connected and constructive way. As we've seen, it is easier to complain, attack, or be passive-aggressive. But we do not get what we want that way. These tactics only make the interaction worse.

Mature honesty creates connection and intimacy through a type of sharing called self-revealing. Stella Resnick, a therapist and author, highlights the power of self-revealing in her book, The Pleasure Zone. She distinguishes self-revealing from self-disclosing, writing that the former creates a more mature kind of intimacy because it involves "discovering yourself anew in the presence of another." When we self-disclose, we present a set story about who we are and why we do things. These stories are based on past ideas and who we have been, rather than allowing ourselves to evolve in each situation we encounter. A self-disclosure response cuts off possibilities, while a self-revealing response creates more possibilities for connection. (Resnick, 1997)

Imagine when a partner makes an invitation to go on a run, for example. One could react with self-disclosure: "I never run. I don't like it." This effectively negates our partner's invitation with a non-negotiable boundary. I will not run because that's not what I do. By contrast, we do not shut down opportunities based on long-held stories about ourselves when we practice self-revealing. Instead, we are open to engage and co-create something new. We could say, "I have not liked running in the past because I got nauseous. But I'm open to talking more about this to see if a short run, or maybe a longer hike, could work."

As we stay present and open to possibility, we honor our partner's requests for company and allow ourselves to discover whether a prior dislike is true. We also learn more about our partner and potentially connect in a deeper way by doing something they enjoy. As we self-reveal, we step into discovery mode. We explore the layers of fear, insecurity, and desire right here and now, rather than assessing, judging, or drawing conclusions. I see this as the "secret sauce" of mature honesty. Not only has revealing vulnerable fears and hurts (rather than invulnerable judgments and blame) saved me from many fights, but it has also created closeness and intimacy that feels simultaneously safe and passionate. My clients, too, report that as they start to reveal more, they experience this new kind of intimacy.

When one of my male clients shared a desire to explore being more submissive in his sex life with his wife, he was met with her self-disclosing response. Her fear and shame about being in a more dominant role caused her to share conclusive ideas about herself that cut off the exploration. "I don't do that," she said. "That's not who I am."

In the shift to self-revelation, moving away from conclusive assessments and instead exploring current feelings, sensations, and thoughts, there is a willingness to discover ourselves anew. If she were willing to do this, his wife's statements would shift to something like, "As you said that, I suddenly felt embarrassed. My stomach clenched. I heard my parents' voices in my head saying sex is dirty and I shouldn't talk about it." Or she could say, "I notice I feel really uncomfortable when I think about your desire. I'm not sure I want to do that, but can we talk about it more?" Self-revealing honesty is the secret sauce because it opens the door for connecting and collaborating, rather than running into a wall or a dead-end.

Self-revealing honesty is a powerful way for couples to bypass stuck dynamics and circumvent painful and distancing judgments and assessments. Self-revealing also brings more aliveness and freshness to a relationship. Over years and decades, many couples feel the staleness of self-disclosure conversations in which we repeat stories about ourselves again and again.

A client recently admitted to being bored when his partner told him about her day (self-disclosing). He also admitted to feeling less excited to have sex as a result of these repetitive conversations. This does not mean we have to avoid sharing our lives with our partners, but we can also start to pay attention to how much aliveness and spark our conversations create. When we want to deepen a connection and reignite passion, it is often time for a self-revealing conversation.

SELF-REVEALING IN ACTION

Self-revealing can happen in and out of the bedroom while initiating or responding to a conversation. I started a self-revealing discussion when I told my partner I sometimes felt alone when we walked together. I shared that I noticed that I felt sad when he walked in front of me. I had held this in for a while because it seemed like such a small thing, but when we arrived at our destination, I would feel disconnected and less attracted to him. I realized that if I kept this to myself, I would stay stuck in this pattern.

Rather than sharing my judgments or accusations: "You walk too fast," OR "You're selfish for not thinking of me when you walk," I tried to be vulnerable instead. I was clumsy as I shared my feelings and desires, but it got through to him. "I notice I feel sad and alone," I said, "when we walk separately. I wonder if you'd be open to walking with me?"

To his credit, he did not take this personally and opened the door to collaboration. He asked more about what would feel good to me. I shared that I felt happy when we walked side by side. And sometimes I liked holding hands. Because I did not attack his character, and he was willing to try something different, we walked home from dinner that night together in a way that felt great to both of us. Win-win!

The benefit of self-revealing honesty is that both partners' needs and desires can be heard and attended to, allowing for collaborative exploration. Resnick writes that self-revealing "redefines intimacy." The way I see it, what people think of as intimacy is often actually compatibility. In the old intimacy paradigm, people would be set up on a date because they both play tennis or like jazz. They seem compatible because they like or do the same things. In the new paradigm, intimacy involves knowing each other more fully and connecting on a more emotional level. When we continue to discover our partner's current excitements, fears, longings, and even pain, passion is more likely to stay alive over time rather than fade after the honeymoon phase.

PRACTICE

Self-revealing honesty can make us feel naked or exposed even with all our clothes on. It is not always comfortable, but the more we do it, the easier it gets. Learning to self-reveal is one of the basic practices that allows for more mature honesty. Let's start accessing your internal layers, so you become more familiar with your more immediate experience, especially your emotions and sensations underneath the default-response stories, judgments, and assessments.

Try this with a friend, partner, colleague, or family member. First, have one person share something they notice about their "internal landscape" – sensations, feelings, or thoughts. To get more practice self-revealing rather than self-disclosing, I suggest prioritizing sharing sensations and feelings as much as possible. If you include thoughts, keep them focused on the current moment rather than drifting into ideas about the future or what happened in the past.

Here are some examples:

I notice...

- My heart is pounding.

- I feel worried.

- My mind is racing. I'm having a lot of thoughts about how different we seem.

The second person responds with: "Hearing you say that, I notice..." and finishes the sentence with something about themselves.

Here are some examples:

Hearing you say that, I notice...

- My stomach clenched.

- I feel happy.

- My thoughts turned to wonder whether you are mad at me.

Set a timer for five minutes to start. Go back and forth with each person doing their best to share their immediate experience.

After the five minutes is over, take some time to debrief by answering these questions:

- What was it like to prioritize sensations and emotions rather than thoughts?

- What was new or different about this experience?

- What shifted between us from doing this exercise together?

For an advanced practice, continue to self-reveal as you debrief the exercise. As you share and listen to each other, pay attention to whether the connection, energy, and vitality between you increases or decreases. Practice describing what you notice to each other.

SHEDDING LIFE-ALIENATING COMMUNICATION

The more we reveal the underlying layers of our experiences, the easier it gets to release blame and accusation, two major drains on intimacy. Bringing our attention to the current moment means we are more likely to notice that the next moment always reveals something new. It is often surprising. At times I have initially felt angry, but upon deeper exploration, I've realized I was afraid or sad. Sadness has transformed into love or longing. Our experience changes moment by moment the more we allow ourselves to be impacted by our own and others' revelations.

The self-revealing practice above is enlivening because neither partner knows where it will go. The unfamiliarity creates the kind of energy couples often experience at the beginning of a relationship — excitement of uncertainty and the unknown.

We benefit from certainty and stability in long-term relationships, but this can kill the passion. Self-revealing can stoke the fire for partners.

Since many couples never learn how to share fears and disappointments without creating blowups, they carry their resentment and hurt, are afraid to talk about what they honestly feel, and then become more distant over time. When you can, as Resnick describes, "discover your feelings in the moment…not explaining or justifying them" and when your partner accepts these feelings with curiosity and tenderness, you can break through to a new level of intimacy. Through this, I see couples feel loved and seen for who they really are, in a way many have never experienced before.

The first few times you try this, it will likely feel awkward, but keep exploring! As my clients and I continue to practice, we find that anything can become a doorway to connection, even upset and awkwardness.

CHAPTER 3

WHO IS BEING HONEST?

———

After I got married, I started hearing words in my mind that were similar to what I had heard my mom say to my dad when I was young. They were sarcastic comments like: "That's how you load the dishwasher?" and "Have you heard of a toilet bowl brush?" I noticed these thoughts and feelings carried a tone and cadence that did not feel like mine. I realized they were not really my thoughts, even though they were in *my* mind and seemed to be reactions to *my* husband! This blew me away.

What we now know is that humans are extremely impressionable from a young age. While we may not imagine our thoughts could come from anyone other than ourselves, there is a process by which we absorb many thoughts from those around us, especially as we are growing up. Nancy Colier is a mindfulness teacher, psychotherapist, and author of four books, including *Can't Stop Thinking*. In her blog post, "Why Our Thoughts Are Not Real," Colier writes that our thoughts are not as personal as we think. "You did not even have the thought you are calling 'yours,'" she writes. "Rather, it appeared to you within your awareness, without you ever choosing it or asking it to show up." (Colier, 2013)

It can be confusing, or even shocking, to consider that we do not choose all the thoughts that arise in our minds. Many thoughts are impressions from our youth that show up in the form of judgments, expectations, and assessments. As we recognize that thoughts arise without choice, we start to be more conscious about which thoughts we believe and which ones we choose to speak aloud.

It takes a strong commitment to speak from the caring and collaborative parts of ourselves, especially when the other voices are louder. While I do not express most of my negative reactions out loud these days, I still hear them in my mind. I hear voices of anger when my partner walks on my yoga mat with his shoes on. I hear voices of nervousness when he spends more money than I want to. I hear voices of irritation when he makes choices that cause him pain. I now pause before I speak, allowing time for the more mature parts to step up. I remember that my judgments are not the whole picture, but they are the echoes of the life-alienating communication most of us have absorbed from our cultural conditioning.

Sometimes it takes a while before I can open my mouth and be proud of what I say. Viktor Frankl, Holocaust survivor and author of *Man's Search for Meaning,* offered this wise re-framing of how we can consciously respond in tense situations: "Between stimulus and response there is space. In that space is our power to choose our response. In our response lies our growth and freedom." With mature honesty, we cultivate the capacity to choose.

WHOSE VOICES ARE IN OUR HEADS?

A powerful and respected framing of the voices in our heads is laid out by Richard Schwartz, PhD, respected psychologist and founder of Internal Family Systems. He discerns that we have a lead "Self" as well as three other types of parts—managers, exiles, and firefighters. Each of these parts has a role to play in an attempt to keep us safe and loved. Exiles are our young parts that hold onto our trauma. They isolate or hide to try to keep us from feeling pain or fear. Managers try to maintain control by doing whatever it takes to avoid rejection or hurt. Firefighters attempt to extinguish "fires" when the exiles get activated, often using addictive or unhealthy methods to counter the exiles' rebellious behavior. (IFS, 2022)

For our exploration of mature honesty, it is enough to understand that each internal part has its own way of thinking and speaking, as well as its own tone of voice and body posture. These parts may even contradict one another. Instead of fighting against these internal fractures, we can learn to accept all of our different parts. Sarah Marshank is a spiritual teacher, author, founder of Selfistry, and a dear friend who has developed a framework called Selfistry, which supports people to get to know and accept all of our selves. At my first Selfistry workshop, Marshank shared a metaphor to clarify what it is like to bring awareness to our many internal selves without judgment. "It's like all of our parts, or selves, are on a bus together," she said. "We do not have to make any part of us wrong, but we get to choose who drives the bus."

The way I see it, we do not want to give the driver's seat—the voice and decision-making power—to the selves who are immature or lean toward self-destruction. We want to give the wheel to the parts whose views and actions have our best interests in mind. As we become more mature, we can witness how inherited thoughts, and the selves that form around them, can sabotage our relationships. When we give the wheel to the parts that believe the self-doubt, righteousness, pessimism, or other unhelpful framings of life, we suffer and so do our relationships.

According to Drs. John and Julie Gottman in their book *10 Lessons to Transform Your Marriage,* we find ourselves in painful relationship dynamics where the "Four Horsemen of the Apocalypse" run rampant—reminder: these are criticism, contempt, defensiveness, and stonewalling (Gottman, 2006). Knowing that we can question our thoughts starts to give us some freedom from being controlled by them.

Marshank's Selfistry framework highlights that each of these selves has value. "Many people wonder," Marshank says, "which self is the real me? I suggest holding off on that decision because they are all valid. We want to get to know them all, rather than get rid of them. We can make room for all the selves within us."

While it can be surprising that thoughts arise in our minds through different parts or sub-personalities, many spiritual teachers and psychologists acknowledge that the cohesive self we seem to have is actually an illusion. Dennis Genpo Merzel, is a Buddhist teacher and creator of the Big Mind/ Big Heart process, a teaching that serves to help us access the wise or awakened mind he believes we all have access to. "Imagine your body-mind-spirit as a company," Merzel writes. "You're a company with many employees, and not one single employee knows his job title, job description, function, what the product is, or who the CEO is. To make matters worse, each employee thinks he's the boss, the one in charge, and all the other employees are working for him." (Merzel, 2008)

As Merzel points out in his book, *Big Mind Big Heart*, the thoughts in our heads are connected to innumerable internal "employees," but we relate to them as though they are all "Me." This is very important for mature honesty because, similar to choosing which thoughts we believe, we can also choose which parts, or selves, we trust to speak for us. For example, I have a fearful, pessimistic part that can take over. When she does the talking, she inevitably creates drama and conflict. It takes effort to be aware of her opinions, desires, and fears without letting them take over a conversation and destroy intimacy. It takes discipline to look for the wiser, more optimistic parts before I open my mouth to speak. Meditation has been an important part of cultivating the capacity to witness, rather than act out these parts. (Merzel, 2007)

Valuing and making room for all of our selves is different from giving all of them power. As we welcome and get to know our inner selves, we realize how many of them there are. Marshank and Schwartz say it's possible there are an infinite number. We all have parts that are angry, scared, and hurt. We have parts that try to protect us and parts that rebel, parts that want connection and parts that crave freedom. As we mature our honesty, we recognize which parts are more trustworthy than others, and we give those parts more power.

During a recent Selfistry workshop, where we played with expressing the various selves through embodied movement practice, art, and inquiry, Marshank guided us in a "constellation exercise." This meant that other participants acted out the patterns of *my* inner selves, allowing me to witness them outside my mind. This bird's-eye view brought powerful insights as I saw how my past experiences came to create my present-day personality. I became more familiar with many of my parts, including the fearful pessimistic part of me that Marshank lovingly labeled my "Curmudgeon." As a result, I am better able to take these parts' perspectives into account with compassion, but without letting them drive the bus. While I can validate the intensity of their emotions, I buckle all of my immature parts into passenger seats and call on a more mature part to drive.

WE ARE NOT WHO WE THINK WE ARE, AND NEITHER ARE OUR PARTNERS

After my divorce, I made a commitment to speak from the selves who would create more connection and steer conversations toward the highest good for everyone involved. I decided that during conflict, I would not speak until I could say something I would not regret. I developed the awareness to notice my Curmudgeon's thoughts through mindfulness and meditation practices. And, similar to Merzel's Big Mind/Big Heart process, I found I could ask the more mature selves to weigh in when my younger parts were activated. The practice of consciously choosing which self to give the driver's wheel has allowed me to create more loving, collaborative, and connected relationships and to guide my clients to do the same. What I've found is that less energy gets drained through conflict, so couples have more energy for play, intimacy, and passion.

Another psychologist with a framework that helps us understand which inner parts are responsible for unsatisfying situations is

Terry Real. Real created a form of couples counseling called Relational Life Therapy. Relational Life Therapy adds to traditional therapy by teaching skills for living relationally—connecting with oneself through one's thoughts, feelings, sensations, and others. He distinguishes the Adaptive Child from the Wise Adult. In his work with couples, he believes getting clear about which part a person speaks from is as important, or even more important, than the content of a fight. (Real, 2018)

When we speak from our Adaptive Child, we see through lenses that make things look black or white, right or wrong, always or never. We tend to make assumptions and react from fear, which cuts off our flexibility, creativity, and ability to collaborate. When we speak from the adult self, we have more access to subtlety, discernment, and curiosity. This was apparent in a couple I coached when they had a baby, and they were struggling to feel connected. They came to me feeling overwhelmed and frustrated, recounting a recent fight:

Vishan admitted he was tense and irritated when he asked Angelique to clean up the baby's highchair tray before they went to bed. His request was loaded with upset. As they recounted the incident, Angelique admitted she had responded in an equally irritated tone. "Sure," she had said, covering up her hurt with anger. "And how about cleaning up your dessert bowl that's still on the counter?"

They each felt hurt by the other, even though they agreed the content of their argument did not seem like a big deal. They asked me to help them understand the dynamic so they could feel connected again. I asked Angelique to speak freely, setting aside her worry about hurting Vishan's feelings. Vishan agreed we could welcome the part that was upset and give it a voice because she frequently held in upsets and disappointments. They both knew this resulted in bigger conflicts at a later time. The part that can be vulnerable and communicate its needs with sovereignty and respect—the Big Mind, functional adult, mature part, and so on—is often blocked by the younger, more emotionally volatile part. Having a facilitator to assist is helpful.

"I don't like when you talk to me like I'm an employee, as if your way is the right way and the only way," she said. "I spend all day with our kid. I am exhausted at the end of the day, and I give myself a break and don't wipe the tray and *that's* what you get pissed at me for? How about some appreciation for what I've done *all* day?" she sobbed.

I guided Vishan to "step into her shoes" and respond from his adult self, reflecting what he heard. He did a great job. "I can see that I have lots of ideas about how to be more efficient," he said, "and I need to remember that you have a different way of doing things. You are exhausted at the end of the day, and I hear that you need me to cut you some slack."

"Yes," she said emphatically. "I know you like hacking your life and performance, but I don't want to be hacked."

"I know," Vishan said, dipping into his more emotionally volatile parts. "But it is frustrating to me when the highchair is dirty in the morning and I go to feed the baby on my way to work. It takes extra time, and then I run late."

Now we were getting into the underlying issues they each had. The surface upset was about cleanliness, but deeper than that, they each felt unappreciated and unsupported in what they were doing—Angelique for spending full days with the baby, and Vishan for his morning childcare.

I asked if, when the argument happened, they had communicated the parts about feeling under-appreciated. They said they had not. This is very common, to react emotionally when upset, rather than taking the time to find and speak from a mature part. I asked if hearing that they both felt vulnerable changed what they felt about each other.

They both said yes. Instead of seeing an enemy or critic, the vulnerability humanized them. "I want to support you," Angelique said. "Hearing that you're struggling, rather than picking at me for doing something wrong, helps me understand you." "Yes," Vishan said. "And it helps to remember all the things you do all day for our baby." As their primal reactions from feeling attacked and criticized settled down, they started to see the person they loved sitting across from them again!

WE HAVE A PAIN-BODY THAT DISTORTS HONESTY

Spiritual teacher and author, Eckhart Tolle, teaches another framework that illuminates how we speak from different parts. His framing identifies that all humans have a pain-body. The pain-body holds onto the emotional pain from our life experiences. In his book, *The Power of Now,* Tolle writes "when we are unable to be present, or to access the power of the Now, every emotional experience leaves a residue of pain that lives on in you." (Tolle, 1999)

This residue is the root of our blaming, shaming, and attacking others. Our current experiences, he writes, "merge with the pain from the past, which was already there, and has become lodged in your mind and body." This is why, for instance, my fight with my ex-husband about the water bottle—in the introduction section of this book—was so intense. All the fear and scarcity from my past came barreling into the moment we considered buying a twelve-dollar bottle, even though it wasn't the bottle that enraged me. It was just like when my parents fought about time management. They were working out a much deeper conflict.

Now that I am aware of my multitude of selves, I practice giving voice to those who are able to be vulnerable and see at least two sides to every story. These are the parts that are not caught in the pain-body and help us create harmonious, connected relationships. Asking ourselves questions like "What would it take to let go of thinking my way is the right way?" and "What is vulnerable for me about this situation?" can help us access our more mature parts. If we are not willing or able to answer these questions, I suggest giving ourselves a "time-out." Whether it is a few minutes or a few days, we have much better outcomes when we do not speak from our pain-body.

Conflict and tension occur when our anxious and fearful parts run the show. As we get frustrated and angry with our partners, we are more likely to react from the younger parts—our pain-body and Adaptive Child parts—than we are to respond to the current moment. This distorts our honesty and leads us to speak in life-alienating ways. Learning about our psychological and spiritual nature helps us break habits and thought patterns that are stuck, resentful, and disconnected. Using the space Frankl speaks of to slow down and choose our responses, creates a relationship with more honesty and love.

EXPLORING THE SELVES IN RELATIONSHIP

Shirzad Chamine, chairman emeritus and former CEO of the largest professional coach training organization of the world, the Co-Active Training Institute, is the creator of Positive Intelligence Coaching. His method also guides us to become more conscious of our parts. He distinguishes the "Saboteur" mind from the "Sage" mind. The Saboteur mind directs our fearful, arrogant, and controlling behaviors. The Sage mind, by contrast, is much more compassionate, spacious, and forgiving. It sees that everything can be turned into a gift or an opportunity.

As I trained to become a certified Positive Intelligence Coach, I learned about what Chamine calls the "self-command muscle." This is our ability to recognize when we are caught in the Saboteur mind and take steps to shift into the Sage mind. His framework gives us yet another way to practice speaking from parts of ourselves that create more connection, respect, and trust. When a client was upset that his partner was not checking in about important events he had coming up, I had him practice speaking from his Sage mind. We saw that as he stewed about why his partner did not ask questions about his week, a part of him was hurt. This part, expressed through his Saboteur mind, speculated that either his partner (1) did not care, (2) was so focused on her own life that she selfishly could not be bothered with what was going on in his, or (3) did not respect his work, and thus did not ask about it.

He agreed that the sad and angry parts were Saboteur parts. A telltale sign was their desire to lash out and pull away. While the young Saboteur parts wanted to give up on the relationship, I guided him to wait to speak until he accessed the part of him that knew he could navigate their different styles and needs. The more mature parts look for ways to create connection, even amid pain and disappointment.

It took some guidance to access his Sage mind, the part that felt care and curiosity about the situation. I supported him in a meditative inquiry into what felt more vulnerable than the anger and upset. It turned out, as it often does when we look deeper, he was afraid. Once we found the fear, he was able to reveal it, rather than rush to blame her. He shared the vulnerability he found, telling her he was afraid that asking for support made him seem weak and unlovable. Instead of blaming or attacking her, I helped him shift the conversation to get curious about her. He set aside his stories about what he thought she was thinking to find out what she was actually thinking.

As he asked questions, she let him know she was committed to supporting him. Yet he had appeared so calm, cool, and collected that she didn't realize he needed her. She apologized and acknowledged she could see that asking for support was making him feel vulnerable. She agreed to look out for this and lovingly asked if, going forward, he would be willing to open up to her, rather than act so independent. Then she took out her calendar and made sure she could take him to his doctor's appointment. This repair conversation brought them closer than ever because he revealed his vulnerability and opened up to her for support.

An example from my own life highlights the power of exploring our various selves. It was a poignant night for me and my partner. I was about to take a solo trip for two months to figure out whether I was going to move out of the area. We both knew this could potentially end our relationship. While this was my choice, the Saboteur voice in my head was irritated and resentful. This part blamed him for not co-creating the family dynamic I wanted, where we spent time with all of our kids. If we had this, the voice said, I would not be considering moving away.

The Sage voice had a different story. That part knew my partner was doing the best he could with his own family dynamics. He had older kids, which meant we were in different phases of parenting. My Sage mind knew I had no idea what it was like to have teenagers. As I looked at him, I heard both selves in my mind. I saw that I could choose to speak from the resentful part or the part that had compassion for him. I could choose which part I would allow to drive the bus.

The young parts often want to be the ones to talk when we are upset. They have a lot to say, which is similar to young children who cannot contain their emotions. But with my commitment to hold off speaking until I could bring clarity and care, rather than instigate more pain, I paused and regrouped. Instead of speaking from the bitter, hopeless parts, I spoke from a mature and vulnerable part. "I can imagine it is not easy to integrate teenage children into a new romantic relationship after a divorce," I said. "And it is really hard for me that we don't spend any time with all of our kids together." Rather than hiding behind a protective wall or lashing out, I shared the sadness in my heart while also acknowledging his struggles.

The vulnerability became a doorway to connection, as often happens when we admit our pain, rather than act it out. He let me know our situation was painful for him too, and he felt sad because his efforts had fallen flat. He said he would continue to see how he could help make this part of our relationship feel good to me. As a result of this conversation, I came to the realization that what was more important than all of us spending time together was having family time with him and my kid. From then on, he started spending more time with us. This situation reminded me that even the most painful experiences can be talked about with care and curiosity.

FAMILIARIZING OURSELVES WITH THE VOICES IN OUR HEADS

Until we question the voices in our head that blame, shame, and attack others, we have very little hope of creating a thriving, lasting relationship. When clients come to me, many do not realize how often we speak from our pain-body, Adaptive Child, and Saboteur parts, especially when we feel hurt. Most of us were never taught to access the Sage mind, Wise Adult, and more mature and wise parts.

For those who have never heard voices in their minds, becoming aware of them can be startling. Some people hear words, while others are aware of bodily sensations, including tension, heaviness, or a shrinking feeling. While the first response to noticing these may be fear or discomfort, the more you listen, the more you will become empowered to choose your responses, rather than ending up stuck in self-sabotaging patterns. In the practice section, I will reiterate how to shift from unconscious reactions to conscious responses.

We all have parts that collapse and freeze, parts that manipulate and deny, and parts that wish for others to hurt when we hurt. This is part of our human psychology. When we stop judging ourselves for having these parts and instead openly explore them, they stop controlling us. As we compassionately witness, rather than act out our parts, we gain access to their underlying concerns.

I once guided a client who was feeling tense to see which part of her was feeling upset. We found a part that was worried about money. She was in the midst of making financial decisions with her partner, and it was bringing up old money fears. We lovingly asked this part why she was so upset. This part's first response was one of righteousness and anger. She wanted things her way, and she was ready to put up a fight. We continued the conversation with this part, acknowledging that her feelings were okay and asking if she would tell us more. It only took a few minutes for her to reveal fear, sadness, and a lack of feeling safe. Her words were like that of a young child, with very black-and-white thinking.

As we listened with care and curiosity, she softened. We were able to find the vulnerability and desire her protective reaction was covering up. While this was not yet an external agreement or solution with her partner, accessing the vulnerable part meant she could go back and collaborate, rather than freak out on him.

It is important to note that while we do not want the young, fearful selves to run the show or drive the bus, they do need a safe place to express their pain and upset. Most couples do not have enough experience holding space for this kind of expression with their partners. They end up taking it personally or feeling hurt themselves. This is where coaches, therapists, spiritual guides, and energy or body workers are useful. We can use words, sound, and body movements to release tension and pain from the mind, heart, and body. Doing this with someone we are not romantically involved with can help us express and release more freely.

PRACTICE

In this chapter, we've deconstructed the idea of one cohesive self with the help of a variety of experts attesting to the fact that we are made up of multiple parts or selves. This can be a disorienting revelation, but many of my clients have found that it becomes freeing and empowering. It helps normalize the fact that we have inner conflict. We no longer have to believe we are flawed because of any one of our parts. As Marshank said, it is important to welcome and get to know them all. The labels are not as important as recognizing that our young, immature parts throw our nervous systems into states of fear, righteousness, disempowerment, and hopelessness. When we alter our decisions and actions to align with these states, we lose the capacities the mature parts bring—creativity, resilience, compassion, and vision, to name a few. The mature parts also help us communicate our needs in respectful and collaborative ways.

As you pay more attention to your thoughts and their tone, you will notice that the pessimistic and shaming thoughts are your Saboteur and Adaptive Child parts. Encouraging and optimistic thoughts are your Wise Adult, Big Mind, or Sage parts. As you learn to witness these parts, you can slow down your tendency to react. You can pause before you speak. This allows you to communicate with mature honesty and create connections that strengthen over time.

As a reminder, witnessing can be as simple as taking a few breaths and creating some space between the stimulus and the response, as Frankl describes. You can also ask yourself whether you (or the parts that are expressing) can see beyond the right-wrong framing and find what is vulnerable about your pain. You can ask to hear from your Big Mind or Sage mind as well. You may not get clear answers right away, but as Merzel wrote in his book *Big Mind Big Heart:* "What blew my mind, and keeps amazing me, is that just about everyone, whether accomplished Zen student or absolutely new to spiritual practice, is able to access these transcendent voices, and speak clearly and precisely, with complete sincerity about their experience of these voices."

ACCESS COMPASSIONATE HONESTY
FROM THE MATURE PARTS

To help access compassion and maturity, we have to acknowledge our judgments, rather than ignore them. Start by writing down three to five judgments you have about a partner, or someone you care about, in the judgment column.

Next to the judgment, take a guess about which part the judgment comes from. Do not worry about a right answer. You could name a particular part you possess, like Marshank named my Curmudgeon. Or you could simply label it as the Adaptive Child or Saboteur. The point is not to get the right name, but to practice shifting your thoughts to those that are more compassionate by recognizing that a part, rather than all of you, holds judgments.

Next, look at your judgment and find a more compassionate thought that honors the other's struggles and humanity. Write it in the third column. Remember, some of our parts are loud and speak up quickly. Take some time to wait for the quieter voices to also contribute.

Judgment	The part holding it	A more compassionate thought

Making this list not only fosters compassionate thinking, it also helps you start to get to know your parts. Continue paying attention to the various parts as you have conversations, especially the ones where you feel hurt. Practice slowing down and making the choice to speak from your mature parts, the ones that want the best for you and everyone involved. I guarantee this will give connection and intimacy a better chance to flourish.

CHAPTER 4

HOW HONEST ARE YOU WITH YOURSELF?

One night, in my late thirties and post-divorce, I sat in bed alone, tears rolling down my face, answering the question *"What have I not been honest about with myself today?"* I knew my romantic relationship at the time was not going well, but I was afraid to admit it, and a part of me was committed to avoiding this realization. I was nearing forty as the mother of a young child. I wanted to have another kid and was afraid to let go of this relationship, both because my biological clock was ticking and because I did not want to hurt or upset him. While it was initially surprising to see that I could avoid knowing my truth, I saw how masterfully I had been pushing it aside.

I learned to ask myself this question from a friend who was training to be a coach after decades of taking personal growth workshops. He recommended I answer it every night because he knew me so well. At that point, in my twenties, I self-identified as a people pleaser and spent much of my life trying to make others happy. I put aside my desires when I thought they would upset anyone. Preferring to let something slide rather than speak my mind created trouble for me in relationships. After months, or years, of ignoring or disowning my truth, I would become bitter, resentful, distant, or explosive.

People pleasing and codependent tendencies are common among my clients and friends. While I hear many complaints about selfish daters and lovers, I hear as many complaints about partners who seem meek or ghostlike in their attempt to be good or kind. People pleasing starts at a young age as parent pleasing. Many parents unknowingly show more love when their kids act in ways parents deem respectful and responsible and may be standoffish and inconsistent with their affection when they see behavior they don't like. This teaches kids that they need to prove themselves to receive love. [2] As a parent, I know it is a Herculean task to consistently guide kids toward self-confidence, courage, and the ability to connect with others. Though we have great intentions, we undoubtedly pass on our fears and wounds, often without even realizing it.

The need to prove oneself is not reserved for those who endured traumatic parenting experiences. Most of us were—knowingly or unknowingly—persuaded to live out our parents' agendas for success or happiness. We thus lost sight of at least some of our own sovereignty and inner knowing. Even though I grew up in a loving family, taking on the role of peacemaker in my home caused me to play out this role in a wider sphere

---

2   Patricia Williams really explores these ideas in her article "This Is Why We Become People Pleasers."

as well. Outside my home, I had a strong desire to be liked. As I got more honest with myself, I started to see how many of my behaviors were conditioned by people pleasing.

As I sat in bed exploring what I had not been honest with myself about, I wrote things like:

- I packed my schedule too full and exhausted myself this week. Why do I work so hard?

- My feelings were hurt when [Name] did not ask about my important meeting. I don't know how to say so, but I know it will build resentment if I don't.

- I was angry when [Name] told me I should try to relax. I felt misunderstood.

Getting more honest with myself has allowed me to be honest in relationships. In her book *Please Yourself*, author and psychotherapist Emma Reed Turrell stresses that she will help us "get better at being disliked, instead of staying quiet," help us find "acceptance instead of avoidance and [. . .] grow instead of staying small." Each of these shifts is based on being honest with ourselves, rather than hiding our truth. We can show up in relationships knowing what we want and communicating it, rather than holding back in fear. I have often been in romantic relationships with other people pleasers. Together, we would work to counter our tendency to be overly nice. As we got more honest with ourselves, we could call each other out on our *"I'm sorrys"* and *"only if it works for yous,"* so we would not lose ourselves. (Turrell, 2021)

DO YOU UNKNOWINGLY HIDE YOUR TRUTH FROM YOURSELF?

Avoiding honesty with ourselves can be done in many ways. I have a history of thinking I will be a burden or high maintenance if I have needs. My needs seem to disappear behind a fog in my mind. Because I don't want others to think I'm "too much," something as simple as feeling cold and wanting a blanket has brought up the fear that someone would feel bothered by me. At times, I have allowed myself to be cold, instead of asking for what I wanted. Even those who are clear and capable of consistently standing up for themselves and asking for what they want can avoid their honesty. From the outside, a strong "this is who I am" or "my way or the highway" personality seems very clear. However, this can be a facade that covers vulnerable truths. Every one of my clients who has tried this self-honesty practice has unearthed important truths from it, whether they thought they were being honest with themselves or not.

As we explore how to create relationships with more honesty, it is clear that relational honesty relies on the willingness to be honest with ourselves. As we explored in Chapter 2, understanding our different selves helps us avoid ending up resentful, depleted, or defeated. Although I cannot guarantee people always stick around when we get honest, I can guarantee that anything we discover can be a doorway to deeper connection. The key is to learn how to have mature, honest conversations.

Many of my clients have gone through the eye of the needle in their relationships and come out on the other side. Some have stayed, while others were left by someone or chose to end a relationship. Whatever the case, the more honest they were with themselves, the better they felt and the more inspiring and meaningful life became. At the root of it, many people stop themselves from being honest because they fear they will end up alone if they speak their truth. But my clients have told me, and I know firsthand, that losing oneself in a relationship is also lonely and painful.

Amir is a great example. When he first came to me for coaching, he was not sure whether to stay with his wife. They had not had sex in years, and she had not been loving toward him for a long time. He said he could not imagine being in another relationship, but the pain was becoming so great that he was getting more honest with himself and considering leaving. He could not see himself being able to love or be attracted to another woman, though. He was afraid women would not want him. I was confident that when he started to date again, he would experience deeper connections and more respect, but he did not yet believe it.

Even so, he took a risk that was not easy. It is common to feel the pain of big life changes, but when they allow us to live more aligned with our integrity, we feel better about ourselves. As Amir became more honest with himself, he acknowledged his relationship was full of toxic behavior and it was time to get out. Even though he was afraid he might be alone forever, he knew he could not live this way anymore.

As he went through the separation, he faced his self-doubt. His self-image was skewed by decades of reflection from a "warped mirror." His wife's blame and attack were an example of the "saying it like it is" honesty that can be heartless and irresponsible. As she belittled him, she allowed herself to speak from her young parts, rather than her mature ones. He wondered if what she said was true. Getting more honest with himself allowed him to see that his inner critic was in a nearly constant self-attack mode. While it was painful to see, he started practicing having more compassion for himself.

The changes allowed him to have a more loving relationship and be a positive role model for his kids, which was one of the most important parts of his decision. A few months after the separation, he met a woman at a coffee shop, and they hit it off. I had tears in my eyes as he told me about their first few dates. "Instead of getting dirty looks when I try to do nice things for her, I was appreciated. Instead of trying to get away from me, she is excited to see me. Instead of degrading me, she tells me what she likes about me." Getting honest with ourselves allows us to move toward more love and healthy connection.

MORE WAYS TO GET HONEST WITH OURSELVES AND OUR MOTIVATIONS

In addition to reflecting on the question *"What have I not been honest with myself about today?"* another way to get more honest with ourselves is what Dr. Susan Campbell calls a Daily Authenticity Inventory, from her book *Getting Real.* Similar to my self-honesty journaling, Campbell suggests looking back at the end of a day and writing how we did not "show up for ourselves fully today." When we are not honest with ourselves, we prioritize things like looking good or trying not to hurt others. We ignore our needs and truths. For example, when I did not initiate the conversation I wanted to have with my partner, I did not show up for myself. One of my clients told me she would regularly go along with eating food she knew would upset her stomach so she would not seem high maintenance. She would pay for it later and so did her relationship when she spent the night feeling nauseous.

Campbell adds a couple more layers to her inventory. She suggests asking the question, *"If you were to do it over, what would you do or say differently so you did show up fully for yourself?"* This helps us explore what we could do instead. The practice of considering other options trains us to see how we can be more honest with ourselves. When we are outside the heat of the moment, it is easier to imagine other options, and we find wisdom we can draw on in future situations.

Campbell also invites us to consider our reasons for not fully showing up for ourselves. As we explore this, we get a sense of our deeper motivations and vulnerabilities. One of my reasons for not fully showing up for myself has been fear that when someone else suffers, they will not be available to connect with me. When there is an option of where to sleep on a trip, I have put myself in the more uncomfortable sleeping situation so my partner could get a good night's sleep. I was motivated by a fear that if he was grumpy, he would not be able to have fun with me. Knowing I am tough and can handle uncomfortable situations allows me to be generous, but it can also lead me to not take care of myself. If I sacrifice my comfort too often, I become resentful. Realizing this allows me to show up more fully for myself and be honest about my decisions, rather falling into the role of a martyr. The clearer we can be about when we make excuses, the less they unconsciously run our lives and the more easily we can communicate about them. This allows intimacy to flourish.

There is a powerful metaphor that highlights what happens when we are not honest with ourselves and others. Imagine looking at another person through a pane of glass. In the beginning, the glass is clear, and we see each other clearly. Each time we hide or hold back something important, we throw a splotch of paint on the glass. Eventually, the glass becomes full of paint, and we cannot see the other person anymore. The paint, representing our upsets, judgments, and negative stories about others, becomes all we can see. Relationships do not thrive when we see others through the gunk of blame or righteousness.

When we do not speak up, irritation and resentment build. We unintentionally cut off connection, which is often what we fear will happen if we share our truth. While it can be hard to believe that sharing something we are upset about will actually bring more connection, when done with maturity, it clears the glass. We may have to face some fears in the short term, but we strengthen connection in the long term. Practicing mature and self-revealing honesty makes both the short and long term go smoother.

OUR BODIES, GENDER, AND HONESTY

David Whyte, poet and author, writes in his book *Consolations*, "*Where we cannot go in our mind, our memory, or our body, is where we cannot be straight with another, with the world, or with ourself.*" By "*where we cannot go,*" Whyte refers to an inability to know and be honest with ourselves. When we are not aware of our thoughts, emotions, or bodily sensations, we cannot consciously share them with others. Sadly, many of us are culturally conditioned out of honesty, even with ourselves. Boys from a young age are encouraged to "man up" and hide their feelings of insecurity and fear. Sports coaches and parents often guide them to suck it up and avoid showing emotion at all costs. As a result, men are trained to bypass what they feel. (Whyte 2020)

A male client who found out his wife had an affair told me he had been the tough guy growing up. When he found out about the affair, he had many feelings he said he "wasn't supposed to feel." Our conversation went like this.

"I think I'm sad," he said.

"I would be shocked if you weren't," I said.

"I want to get past this ache so I don't feel weak. I want to feel powerful again," he said.

"I understand," I said. "The way you will get back to your true power is to start with feeling the pain, rather than trying to ignore it. Even though you've been conditioned to believe that aches and pain are weak and unmanly, they are not, and they are a doorway to your true power."

In Buddhism, there is a distinction between the original suffering we feel about a misfortune and the self-judgment, or analysis, we add on top. The original pain is referred to as the first arrow. Our reaction to pain—the ideas, assessments, and judgments we have about it—is the second arrow. *"In life,"* the Buddha said, *"we can't always control the first arrow. However, the second arrow is optional."*

I guided my client to pay attention to his original emotions and bodily sensations and let go of the second arrows—his judgments and assessments about himself. "I want to get past this ache so I don't feel weak" was a second arrow because he was judging what he was feeling as wrong. On a fundamental level, the Buddha shows that none of our emotions or bodily sensations are wrong or bad. Our first arrows simply arise. Although someone else might not like what arises for us or may feel uncomfortable about it, this does not make our experience wrong.

To my client's surprise, as his awareness expanded beyond his mind's judgments and fear, he felt more of the visceral sensations in his body and began to relax. Even though the sensations did not feel "good," he was experiencing himself beyond the good-bad dichotomy, a framework we use to judge ourselves. After a short time, he said, "I feel a lot more peaceful now." It seemed ironic to him because he was feeling the pain he was originally trying to get rid of. But as we welcomed, rather than judged, his feelings, it became safer for him to be more honest with himself and overcome the old scripts that told him he should "get over it."

I have pierced myself with second arrows too, comparing myself with others and coming up short. Most of my clients do this. But during our sessions, they often say they feel more peaceful. They stop shooting arrows at themselves as they are accepted and guided beyond the second arrows to the original feelings. It can be tempting to ignore our feelings and sensations, but ultimately, it does not go well. This turns into spiritual bypass, a term introduced in the early 1980s by John Welwood, a Buddhist teacher and psychotherapist. Spiritual bypass is the "tendency to use spiritual ideas and practices to sidestep or avoid facing unresolved emotional issues, psychological wounds, and unfinished developmental tasks." When we bypass, we ignore what feels "bad" and are thus not honest with ourselves. (Welwood, 2011)

While women in Western culture are encouraged to be a bit more honest with themselves than men, women are still often shamed for feeling too much or acting too emotional. When I began facilitating workshops for women after having facilitated workshops for men, I thought women would be much more forthcoming with their emotions and honesty. But as we sat in a circle on the first night of a workshop, women were also afraid to reveal their vulnerable thoughts and feelings. Many women said it felt risky to reveal their fears, judgments, jealousy, and disappointments. They were afraid of what others would think.

At first, I was surprised to see women holding back as much as men I had worked with, but my surprise waned as I remembered the shame I have also felt about my vulnerable truths. I thought back to a night in my twenties when I had just been through a breakup of a two-year relationship. My mom, sister, and I were sitting at the kitchen table. I was crying, and they were trying to comfort me by saying "You'll be fine." It was their attempt to be compassionate, and I knew I would be fine at some point, but it was also confusing. My honest experience was a lot more complex than "fine." I wanted it to be okay that I was hurting at that moment. Many families avoid the discomfort of pain rather than welcoming it and saying, "It's okay to feel sad or mad or scared," or "Tell me more about how you're feeling."

With my family prioritizing being "fine," I did not learn to be honest with myself. Over time, it has gotten easier to speak up about my truths, but it may never feel natural. When I get disappointed or hurt, I tend to think I should not be so sensitive. When I want something, I feel afraid it will hurt my partner's feelings or make him feel bad about himself. Patterns from our youth may not go away completely, but with awareness we can share them honestly with a partner and heal together.

PRACTICE

Avoiding our upsets by eating, drinking, shopping, or another vice of your choice is common. However, bringing awareness to your upsets and being honest with yourself will free you from unconscious habits and destructive behaviors. To become more honest with yourself, start to pay closer attention to the moments when you feel uncomfortable or upset. Make a page in your journal or a note on your phone to track them.

First, note what part of the objective situation is upsetting for you. Since many of us spend much of our time in thought, these will likely be your thoughts about the situation. From here, expand your awareness to include your emotions and bodily sensations.

Bodily sensations have been the most challenging for my clients to track. This may be because, in the West, we are not raised to pay attention to our bodies' wisdom, even though there is scientific research that points to our gut as a second brain. Our common expressions reveal this connection between emotion and the body. You may feel like you've been "punched in the gut," or your "heart is in your throat," or "your cheeks are burning," or you "feel like you are spinning." Becoming more aware of these sensations will eventually clarify relationship dynamics, even when they seem random.

I teach my clients the skill of checking in with bodily sensations as a tool for being honest with ourselves and for creating connection. As we become more aware of the visceral sensations of our upsets, we can use the above perceptions, rather than lashing out. "I feel like I was punched in the gut" goes over better than "You're being an asshole!" "My cheeks are burning" creates less defensiveness than "I want to rip your head off." "I feel fear in my chest" will be better received than "I hate when you do that."

Focusing on the body helps us stop blaming and attacking. We become more fundamentally truthful as we keep our attention on the pain of our first arrows, rather than blaming or lashing out at our partners. This becomes the foundation of communicating our needs without apology and collapse on the one hand or defense and rigidity on the other. We grow to trust ourselves and believe in our honesty as we learn to stay in contact with these initial hurts and discomforts. Instead of accusations and bitterness, which create downward spirals of despair, we create upward spirals of hope and intimacy.

Noticing and making notes about your experience is a great tool to start with. Throughout this book, you will learn more tools to make it easier to communicate in ways that create connection, rather than disconnection. For now, fill in the lines below for three to five situations.

Objective situation that is upsetting to me

Example: My partner told me I did something wrong

Thoughts	Feelings	Bodily Sensations
I think she thinks she is better than me	*I feel hurt and angry*	*I shrink and feel tense*

Objective situation that is upsetting to me

Thoughts	Feelings	Bodily Sensations

Objective situation that is upsetting to me

Thoughts	Feelings	Bodily Sensations

Objective situation that is upsetting to me

Thoughts	Feelings	Bodily Sensations

Objective situation that is upsetting to me

Thoughts	Feelings	Bodily Sensations

Objective situation that is upsetting to me

Thoughts	Feelings	Bodily Sensations

When my client returned to a session after practicing this with his wife, he was elated. "This week, when she got upset with me, instead of fighting back and trying to prove it wasn't as bad as she was making it seem, I told her I started feeling sick to my stomach," he said. "When I did not defend and intensify our fight, she actually became concerned about my well-being. We slowed down and had a more rational and connected conversation than we ever have with us feeling upset."

It may seem like a simple shift that would not make such a big difference, but letting go of defensiveness and staying present in the moment allow for connection to happen. Practice this here and take this into your current relationships, romantic and otherwise.

PART 2

CHAPTER 5

APPLYING HONESTY
TO DESIRES

——

"Do you think they give toys to kids on their birthdays?" my kid asked me one day when we had stopped at a drugstore to pick up some candles.

"I doubt it," I said, "but you could ask."

It was around my kid's fifth birthday. As we wandered around, Ari laid eyes on a little gray and white stuffed kitten.

Without missing a beat, Ari proudly strode up to the cashier and asked:

"Do you give toys for birthdays?"

"No, we do not," the cashier kindly replied.

I saw the wheels spinning as Ari considered what to say next and then asked, "Will you do it today for me, even though you don't usually?"

The cashier laughed and thought for a moment. "For you?" he said, "Okay."

Ari was thrilled by this, and I marveled at how easy it can be for kids to ask for what they want. When it does not go their way, they often ask again. At home, I sometimes regret the fact that I have encouraged speaking up about desires. The seventh time I hear a slightly different request to see if I will dispense more candy, I want to pull my hair out. But I am grateful to foster a different relationship with desires than I have. My fear has been that asking, even for little things, will inconvenience or irritate others. This has caused painful dynamics in my relationships.

DESIRE IN ROMANTIC RELATIONSHIPS

Couples often fall into the "pothole" of unrequested desires. My clients tell me about relationship dynamics where one or both partners have not asked for what they want or have given up after asking once and feeling rejected. They then felt a wide spectrum of feelings, from devastation to rage. Speaking desires aloud can feel so risky that they end up unspoken and implicit, rather than spoken aloud and explicit. Sadly, when desires are not fulfilled, people tend to point the finger in blame or want to end a relationship. When we are not getting or co-creating what we want, it is important to honestly look at whether we have effectively asked for it—more than once—rather than hiding or implying our desires.

Our partners may seem unwilling or selfish to us when they are simply unaware. It would be amazing to have a mind reader for a partner, but that fantasy sets us up for major disappointment. And even though it feels awful to blame our partners, it is easier than risking rejection. As we saw in Chapter 3, being honest about our desires can be so scary that we even withhold them from ourselves. So, this is a good time to bring compassion for everyone.

WHAT IF WE WERE LOUD AND PROUD ABOUT OUR DESIRES?

What would romantic relationships be like if we were loud and proud about our desires? Marcia Baczynski has been a friend and colleague of mine for a decade. She is an internationally recognized coach, author, and speaker, focusing on sexual communication, boundaries, and consent. Baczynski works with couples to create healthier sensual and sexual relationships. In her decades of work, she has identified a core issue that keeps people from getting more of what they want in love, connection, and sex. "Many people," she told me, "ask only for what they think they will get, rather than what they really want."

Baczynski's statement opened my eyes as I saw how much asking only for the minimum contributes to my clients' resentment and disappointment. I hear many stories about how partners fall short, but as we look deeper, my clients sometimes realize they have never spoken their desires aloud. This is like going into a restaurant and, without looking at the menu, telling the waiter to bring you whatever they recommend. But then, after receiving the plate of food, you get frustrated with what's there and complain about it.

Of course, we do not hand our partners a concrete menu, but in a way, we and our partners offer a menu of what we know and like. Relationships become much more connected and exciting when we become aware of our "menu" of desires and talk about it. What if, instead of Baczynski's assessment of people asking for about 30 percent of what we want, we asked for closer to 100 percent? We would not get it all, but we would get much more than if we were to hold back our desires.

In a recent coaching session, my client Brenda was not sure if her relationship was going to survive. She tried to have a few "where is this relationship going?" conversations, but her partner was upset by them, so she felt afraid to revisit the topic. With these conversations unresolved, she was on the verge of ending her relationship, even though there were many good reasons to stay together. Brenda knew it was important to her to be able to talk about relationship struggles in an open and honest way, but it seemed her partner could not handle this. One day, she called her partner out of the blue and said: "It's over." Her partner was shocked. Why did she call it off so suddenly without discussing it with him? Why wasn't he informed about how important these concerns were for her and sooner?

Brenda felt like she had tried, but it had not worked to discuss the issues, and it felt risky to keep trying. Looking back on suddenly calling it quits, she realized it was scarier to circle back to the concerns and risk more upset than it was to end the relationship!

I have done this in my relationships too. I remember sitting with a partner in the midst of a disagreement. I said, "Maybe

we should end this. Maybe our relationship just won't work."
He looked at me, managing to keep his cool, and said, "I
think you jumped about seven steps ahead. Why don't you
tell me more about what's frustrating you and what you really
want?" In that moment, he helped me recognize my tendency
to catastrophize, rather than ask for what I wanted during
arguments and misunderstandings.

Why does it feel scarier to me and my clients to be honest
about our desires than to bail on a relationship?

Clients have shown me that being rejected by someone we care
about can feel as frightening as our fears of death and public
speaking. Sharing desires is vulnerable because if someone
says "no," it can seem like they are saying "no" to much more
than the request. It's like they are saying "no" to everything
about us. We may try to get around this by not asking, which is
effectively saying "no" to ourselves before someone else can. If
we end a relationship, we do not have to feel rejected. Ending a
relationship becomes the less vulnerable option that brings clarity and closure to a messy situation we feel we cannot control.

Why is rejection so painful? Through using MRI machines
to scan the brains of people who recalled a recent rejection,
doctors found something surprising. (Roberts, 2020) The
areas of our brain activated when we experience rejection are
the same as when we experience physical pain. This is why
emotions like heartache and grief physically hurt.

Pain is a part of our warning and survival system. The potential
pain of rejection causes us to make decisions we often regret
when we look back. My client felt ashamed for blindsiding her

partner. Her intention was not to hurt him. She had panicked and hit the eject button in an attempt to ease her pain.

In his best-selling book, *Rejection Proof: How I Beat Fear and Became Invincible Through 100 Days of Rejection,* Jia Jang writes about one hundred days of attempting to overcome the fear of rejection that had plagued him since his youth. Jang practiced asking for what he wanted and faced the possibility of being rejected over and over again. His one hundred days started out with silly requests, like asking for a "burger refill" at a fast-food joint and asking if he could plant flowers in a neighbor's yard. (Jang, 2015)

Looking back to his attitude before the experiment, Jang said, "Every time I felt the slightest rejection, I would run as fast as I could." Afterward, he found that running from rejection closes doors that can open if we persevere. Instead of running, we can look inward to the sources of our fear. One major source is looking to others to validate us, rather than validating ourselves. The more we seek external validation, the more the rejection hurts because our sense of self-worth fluctuates based on what others reflect. Learning to validate ourselves gives us a steady foundation from which to play and take more risks. It is easier said than done, but Jang built the foundation of this self-confidence over a few months. My clients do too.

As he experimented, Jang found that a "no" sometimes became a "yes" when he got curious, rather than dejectedly walking away. After an initial hesitation about having flowers in their yard, Jang discovered his neighbor's concern was about cutting underground power lines. When they collaborated to find a safe place, everyone was happy. Jang now teaches people to overcome fear through rejection training. He believes we empower ourselves by exploring how and where our fear of rejection runs the show in our lives. Similarly, I support my clients to face their rejection fears. I help them see what risks are safer to start with, as well as understand the deeper constructs of how our fear of rejection works. Understanding frees us from the mental prison of fear we often keep ourselves in. Becoming more honest when we feel afraid is the first step to releasing fear's grip.

HOW TO GET MORE COMFORTABLE WANTING AND ASKING

People are not always honest with *themselves* about what they want. Cultural and familial norms can block our ability to know what we do and do not like and what does and does not feel good. My self-honesty journaling practice at the end of the day revealed desires I had not been aware of. It revealed things like "I want more time off, but I have been afraid that would mean I'm lazy" and "Last night during sex, I was afraid to ask for what I wanted, so I stayed quiet. It was good enough, but it could have been amazing."

It can be scary to admit what we want for a couple reasons. The first, I call "the gap." Once we know what we want, we become aware of the gap between our current and desired situation. This awareness can lead to feeling worse than the numbness or dissociation of denial, so there can be more pain than pleasure in the short term. A second reason is that once people get clear about desires, they often judge themselves for not having what they want already. People think that if they were good or deserving enough, they would already have what they want.

This shame can simultaneously arise with a desire, muddying the joy and excitement that desire's innate energy brings.

When Baczynski works with her clients to expand their capacity to want and ask for what they want, she has them play a game to get outrageous with their desires. Games and experiments relieve pressure and make exploring new and scary things more fun and less serious. Baczynski guides them to imagine what they would want if they were not holding back. She shared an example of a woman who set aside her fear of being selfish or needy to allow herself to share her desires with her partner. This is what the woman found when she let herself be outrageous:

> What I really want is for you to have an amazingly healthy dinner on the table when I get home from work and have handled the kids' homework. I then want some awesome family time together before *you* put the kids to bed while I take a bath. Then I want to meet up in the bedroom and have you pleasure me for thirty minutes.

It is common to think we are selfish or greedy for wanting what we want. As delightful as these desires seem when I look at this list, I can see why she would feel uncomfortable asking for them! But even though many of us would hesitate to ask for even one of those desires, asking can open up a new world of enjoyment, connection, pleasure, and passion. I asked Baczynski whether sharing many desires can be offensive or off-putting to partners. "Not," she said, "when people are clear they won't get all of it." She points out that not getting all of it is not so bad when we ask for more, rather than settle for less.

This brings us back to the territory of revealing honesty. While the example above focuses on being outrageous, we all have everyday desires and disappointments to navigate with partners. When we come together with mature honesty, we can negotiate about what is important to us and navigate the feelings when desires are not met. The more vulnerable conversations I have, the more satisfying outcomes I have created with my partners. In the tools section, I include support for creating win-win situations, co-creating agreements, and navigating broken agreements.

Some people pride themselves on only asking for what their partner seems available for. It can seem selfish to ask for what we want when it might make a partner uncomfortable. While this could be framed as generosity, I have seen the cost for many couples. It is similar to when I imagined my partner was too tired to have the conversation I desired. I got upset and never gave him a chance. Preemptively altering our desires based on what we think a partner will like creates disconnection. And when people have less connection, affection, or sex than they want, this can become a downward spiral into disappointment and hopelessness. Our "generosity" can actually cause partners to pull away or become stingy with each other. We also miss out on the possibility of hearing an enthusiastic "yes" to our requests.

WE HAVE TO GET CLEAR ABOUT WHAT WE WANT
Baczynski has noticed, with herself and her clients, that it can be "more challenging to figure out one thing you want most, than to want *many* things." For example, it can be hard to narrow down the *one* thing you want to order at a restaurant. Letting yourself want many things before you decide can make it easier. "I might want the prawns with

walnuts," she said, "*and* the firecracker cauliflower, *and* the chicken garlic noodles, *and* dessert, but I may not choose to order all of them!" Allowing ourselves to acknowledge what we want freely, before honing in on one choice, creates a more expanded menu for ourselves and our partners.

Similarly in relationships, putting more of our desires on the table frees us to be creative and playful, rather than feeling the pressure of needing every desire to be met. For many of us, asking for closer to 100 percent of what we want, rather than 30 percent, would be a radical change. Those of us who get stuck in indecision can start small. We can get used to letting ourselves want more and overcome the fear of being selfish or greedy.

We can practice at a grocery store or coffee shop, where decisions are not life-altering, by asking ourselves things like, "Would I rather have tea or coffee?" Deciding among choices makes it easier than finding a desire out of the blue. Applying this idea to relationships, we can ask ourselves *"Do I want more time together or time apart? Do I want more or less affection? More sex or less sex? More of a certain kind of sex and less of another?"* We can let go of the idea that there are right answers and allow ourselves to dream. This makes it more possible and likely for us to have what we want.

Another way I help my clients find desires when they are not readily apparent is by "backing into them." For many of my clients, it is easier to know what they do not want than what they do want. Most of us do not want more disagreements. We do not want less support. We do not want to be misunderstood. When we know what we do not want, we can turn that around and consider what we do want instead. It can be surprising that there is not just one opposite to each desire we don't want. Wanting fewer disagreements could lead to an exploration of agreements we want to create. It could also inspire a conversation about how we could love each other better or what experiences have made us feel safer and more connected. The options are endless.

PRACTICE

Start to think about what you want more of in your relationships. Similar to my exercise where I admitted truths to myself, this is a time to be more honest with yourself. No one else has to know. As you start thinking about your desires, remember that no desire is too small or too big, too weird or too mundane. Finding desires may point to ways you have settled or lost a part of yourself, so be gentle with yourself. You may feel grief or anger. You may become blank or numb. Amid all of this, it is important to shift from judgment to compassion for yourself. Make time to listen to all your parts, not just the ones that speak up quickly. Make space for those that are shy and hesitant.

Make a list of five to ten things or experiences that would be exciting, supportive, meaningful, or pleasurable that you have not yet asked for from a partner. We'll get to the sexier parts in a later chapter, but if they arise, feel free to include them. If you do not currently have a partner, you can imagine a future relationship or consider what you want with a current friend or family member. See if you can allow yourself to be a bit more outrageous with your desires, like the woman in the example above. If you were even a little bit freer than usual, what would you want? If no one would say "no" to you, what would you ask for?

I want . . .

_____

_____

_____

_____

_____

_____

_____

_____

_____

When you are done with your list, take some time to review and imagine the possibility of these desires becoming reality. Then inquire into why you have not asked for what you want. These questions will help you explore.

What am I afraid will happen if I ask for what I want?

_____

_____

_____

_____

_____

_____

_____

_____

_____

Why am I hesitant to ask for what I want?

_____

_____

_____

_____

_____

_____

What is the cost of not having what I want in my life?

Uncovering this information is powerful. When you choose to share your desires with others, you can include these vulnerable parts. Vulnerability is a way to touch others' hearts and inspire them to support you. As I have guided my clients to include their vulnerability as they share their desires, they have felt more understood and gained more support from their partners. Remember to be gentle with yourself as you get more honest. While it can be scary at first, it will ultimately empower you to co-create what is meaningful and exciting for you.

CHAPTER 6

WHAT IS SEX ACTUALLY?

Merriam-Webster's dictionary definition of sex is so limited and outdated that I want to shout from the rooftops, "Are you kidding me? Where are you hiding the actual definition of sex?"

Merriam-Webster defines *sex* as, *a: Sexually motivated phenomena or behavior. b: Sexual Intercourse*; which tells us nothing. My mom was an English teacher and made it very clear that you cannot define a word with the word itself. So, I looked up *sexual intercourse,* thinking there must be a more expansive definition. But *sexual intercourse* is defined as:

1: Heterosexual intercourse involving penetration of the vagina by the penis: Coitus.

2: Intercourse (such as anal or oral) that does not involve penetration of the vagina by the penis.

In this day and age, citing "heterosexual intercourse" strikes me as ignorant. This outdated, gendered, heteronormative, and incomplete interpretation discounts people who are not heterosexual or cisgendered. It also lacks a sense of what sex actually is! The variety and possibility of sexual experience is completely lost here. When I looked up coitus, all I found was:

1: Physical union of male and female genitalia accompanied by rhythmic movements.

This whole trip down the rabbit hole was deeply disappointing. And although most of us do not learn about sex from a dictionary, definitions create a foundation and framework for cultural understanding. Without clear instruction, most of us learn about sex through media, porn, peer interpretation, and personal exploration.

My work with clients has shown me that many people have never experienced an honest sex life: in terms of knowing what sex actually can be and in being honest about personal desires and preferences. I see people orienting toward a "finger-painting version" of sex, using only a few colors, textures, and shades. What is possible is a "masterpiece version" with a much wider range of color and depth.

One of the wiser teachers I have encountered on this topic is Evelyn Birnbaum, an eighty-year-old spiritual teacher and guide. She has spent thirty years teaching one of the most respected spiritual curricula of our time—the Diamond Approach. I attended a lecture called "Barriers to Pleasure," where she reflected on human sexual tendencies.

"Sex," Birnbaum said, "is much more than what most of learned growing up. There are so many different kinds and degrees and depths of sexual pleasure for human beings that most of us don't know about or ever experience," she said. "We tend to believe that all we know is all there is. This is a shame." Birnbaum has had a rich, and some would say wild, life. In addition to studying the Diamond Approach, she spent decades studying other spiritual traditions, including Osho, a highly controversial teacher and leader of the Rajneesh movement in the 1970s. Osho wrote hundreds of books, including one called *From Sex to Superconsciousness*. His teachings guide students to experience sex as a meditation and a method of transcendence and transformation.

Osho, Birnbaum, and other teachers point to how our conditioned habits limit intimacy and sexual satisfaction. Conditioning dulls pleasure and connection. It causes us to think we need to be better, stronger, last longer, and live up to others' expectations. It is then easy to feel ashamed when we do not feel sexually satisfied or are not satisfying another. Shame leads us to hide our honesty and try to reach the unattainable goal of a continually hot, perfect sex life that porn and rom-coms depict.

The map of sex that many of us stumble upon is akin to finding a single trail through a million-acre national forest. Even if this path leads us through beautiful trees, we are not seeing the variety of the other 95 percent of the forest. We may not even realize the rest of the forest exists.

SHIFTING THE PARADIGM AND GETTING MORE HONEST ABOUT SEX

As previously noted, my eighth-grade sex education class was taught from within this limited paradigm. I learned about fallopian tubes and how to put a condom on a banana for safer sex. No one talked about emotional connection or being present, let alone opening to another's energy body, or reaching beyond bodies to transcendent realms. Belgian psychotherapist Esther Perel is the author of a well-known book called *Mating in Captivity*. In her TED Talk, *The Secret to Desire in Long Term Relationships,* she speaks to a more expanded view of sex: "Sex is not a thing you do," she says. "It's a place you go. It's a space you enter, inside yourself and with another, or others." (Perel, 2014)

Sex is not just genital contact or a physical act. We enter into a relational "space" where we can access the fullness of our senses, the depth of our hearts, and even the permeability of our souls. Each experience can be uniquely healing, transformative, and meaningful. As we release the pressure we put on ourselves, and stop trying to do it right, we can revel in the delight of our senses. We can explore the emotional, energetic, and transcendent dynamics that excite us.

Beyond the genetic imperative to pass on our genes, sex becomes a kind of play—a way to experience pleasure, intimacy, release, connection, aliveness, fascination, and novelty. Many people miss out on the richness and discovery of honest intimacy and sex because they have a limited sense of what is possible and because of the fear of being rejected when we share our vulnerable truths.

Perel poses powerful questions in her talk. "What comes out in you?" she asks. "What parts of yourself do you connect to? What do you seek to express there?" In my experience, these are the questions we want to ask, not just once but again and again. When we inquire honestly into what we want from sex, we get more of what we want. Posing similar questions to my clients, I have found that many have never considered these ideas.

As we discover more about ourselves, doors open to new kinds of sexual experiences. We can transcend our identities and senses of self. We can explore relational and power dynamics. We can use sex to transform stuck-ness and manifest visions. And we can access spiritual realms with a partner and beyond. Sex, it turns out, has a much wider range than most of us were taught, with the potential for play, intimacy, and spiritual experiences.

AN UPDATED, HONEST DEFINITION OF SEX

When we expand our definition and understanding of sex, not only are we likely to have more of it, but we start to discover new possibilities. Beyond goal-oriented intercourse is a new universe of exploration. Many of my clients end up having better sex lives simply from expanding their view of sex. They feel safer to imagine and explore a wider range of experiences, sexual styles, and erogenous zones. These ideas then enter into their conversations and eventually their experiences.

Sex also gets better as we are willing to embrace the honesty and vulnerability of our humanity. When we are not trying to prove ourselves to be right or good enough in our sex lives, we are more available to each other. Masks and facades fall away, and we can be truly intimate. Honest intimacy keeps sex connected and evolving, allowing us to love and be loved by our partners in profound ways.

My clients ask incredulously:

- *I can enjoy sex without orgasm?*

- *I can have sex without an erection?*

- *My whole body can orgasm, not just my genitals?*

- *Sex can be energetic, not just physical?*

- *Eye gazing and breathing together can be as pleasurable as genital contact?*

- *I can release stuck energy and trauma through sex?*

The answer to all of these is yes!

The new definition of sex I propose has a foundation of exploration. Rather than striving for a climax, we can let go of the goal and focus on the experience. Curiosity becomes the guide. Honest sex is about waking up our senses and hearts. We become more mindful and aware, and we can take delight in one's own and others' bodies, hearts, and spirits. Beyond a rote definition of how body parts engage (i.e., Webster's definition of moving genitalia in rhythmic movements), sex is a way to explore pleasure and connection through as much of ourselves as possible. Honest sex is a curious exploration of pleasure and intimacy without an agenda or goal orientation.

HONEST SEX IN ACTION

A client told me about a sexual experience with her partner during which they never took their clothes off. They allowed their bodies to connect and move with the flow of the moment. It was as if they were not moving themselves, but they were being moved, she said. As they breathed together it turned into a kind of dance, even as they were lying down. She felt the energy of a snake in her body, and her movements were slippery and fluid. He felt the energy of a panther in his body and moved with strength and agility. They let go of self-consciousness and allowed their bodies to move together in a spontaneous rhythm. There was no genital climax, but the heightened energy of the whole experience was primal and passionate. After it wound down, they remained elevated. They felt more openness and love in their hearts for days after.

This is one possibility of what happens as we let go of our limited maps of sex. Setting aside self-consciousness allows loving, primal, and expanded energies to flow through us. There is no way to know what will happen, but the willingness to engage in the unknown is often thrilling and new. Our bonds deepen with our partners because we expand from mental knowledge about each other—ideas, history, values— to visceral experiences of each other—in our body, heart, and soul. Finding words to describe this is challenging, but when we are more present and aware—letting go of shoulds and expectations—we can experience a depth of love and excitement that bonds us deeply.

Sex cannot be done wrong, as long as we feel good about it. And I dare say that no matter what we have experienced, more is possible. Every moment is unique, and we are always evolving, which means new and different experiences can always happen. Having practiced yoga for twenty-five years, I continue to open up to more possibilities for my body, breath, and awareness in each class. I have racked up more hours doing yoga than having sex, and for this reason alone, I see that we never reach the end of what is possible. There are many more reasons why this is true as well. As we continue to discover ourselves and our partners, we find that each moment is full of different flavors of connection and pleasure.

SEX AS A PRACTICE

Jamie Wheal is a peak performance expert and the author of *Recapture the Rapture: Rethinking God, Sex, and Death in a World That's Lost Its Mind*. His focus on human performance has led him to explore sex as a practice for expanding consciousness and navigating the challenges of romantic relationships. "Show up on the mat . . ." Jamie said when he joined me on the *Man Alive* podcast for an episode entitled "Guerilla Tantra and the Sexual Yoga of Becoming." Many tantra teachers share the view that showing up on the mat is similar to the framing we hold with meditation, yoga, and martial arts. Showing up on the mat means that we do our practice, whether we feel like it or not. (Wheal, 2019)

Showing up on the mat in a sexual partnership means we bring everything we have and feel to our place of connection, whether it be a bed or another sacred space. We may not feel turned on, but we can still connect and be intimate with a partner, especially with the freedom created by the expanded definition of sex. If we do not want to focus on physical touch, we can connect our hearts and energy. So, no matter what happens physically, we can co-create nourishing and exciting experiences.

Jenny Wade, PhD, author of *Transcendent Sex*, writes: "There really is something better than sex—by orders of magnitude. And it doesn't leave sex behind. It is lovemaking that shatters reality, opens new dimensions, rips the veil between the worlds, and produces ecstasies a thousand times more powerful than the most exquisite orgasm." From my view, Wade describes what sex actually is. Our definition has been so limited, however, that she was inclined to label these experiences as "beyond sex." My hope with this chapter is to release us from the box that limits our understanding of sex and keeps many people suffering. (Wade, 2004)

In another *Man Alive* podcast episode titled "Impotence Could Be the Best Thing That Ever Happened to You," Michael Russer talks about how losing his erection after cancer treatments opened up his sex life in a way that could not have happened if he could stay erect during sex. With his current partner, Michael explores whole-body, whole-being sex. This is possible because our whole body (including our energy field) is an erogenous zone. Taking advantage of this can free men who feel ashamed when they do not have an erection. Genital penetration, while one of the most common sexual activities in heterosexual relationships, is not needed for many sexual practices. (Russer, 2020)

Jordan Gray, relationship coach and another former *Man Alive* podcast guest, also agrees that "sex is about feeling and connection, not about doing or performing." In his article, "33 Ways to Have Sex without an Erection," he lists sexual activities that go beyond intercourse and even beyond focusing on our genitalia. He includes taking a bath together, sharing fantasies, cuddling, extended make-outs, eye gazing, and syncing breath. Sex beyond the limited definition has an endless range of delightful possibilities. (Gray, 2020)

WHAT ELSE IS POSSIBLE?

Many of my clients want more in their sex lives. When I moved to San Francisco in 2000 to study psychology and spirituality, I had no idea I had entered a resurgence of the free love and personal growth movements of the 1960s. My eyes were opened to a more expanded view of sex. I attended communication workshops where participants gazed into others' eyes and shared vulnerable truths. I attended Baczynski's Cuddle Parties, where we practiced honoring ourselves by learning to set boundaries during platonic cuddling. I witnessed a wide range of kinks and fetishes walking around the Folsom Street Fair—a sex- and kink-positive celebration. I learned practices to expand orgasmic potential. I even went to sex parties where singles and couples explored a variety of relational dynamics and partners. I saw a range from the sacred to the profane, and I began to see it all as sacred.

Having my eyes opened to what else was possible as I witnessed the freedom others gave themselves liberated me from the cultural ideas and expectations I had absorbed. I began to discover what actually turned me on and what turned me off. I made peace with the part of me I mentioned earlier who feared being called both a slut and a prude. I accessed a deeper self-love and confidence that allowed me to be more intimate in my relationships since I was not trying to hide parts of myself.

Without knowing what we do and do not want, we cannot communicate or collaborate with a partner, which decreases our sexual satisfaction. Of course, not all of these experiences are a fit for everyone. But as we give ourselves permission to discover what types of sexual exploration call to us, we add depth and excitement to our sexual relationships. Here are a few potential explorations my clients and I have found to be particularly transformative.

TANTRA

Tantra is an Indian practice that is more than five thousand years old. In its depth, the study of tantra includes ancient teachings for a balanced and well-lived life, as well as meditation, yoga, mantras, rituals, and teachings about sex. Tantra is the practice of opening our senses, awareness, and emotions to fully experience life. It is about bringing openness and presence to each moment to create more aliveness.

In the context of sex, tantra weaves the physical with the spiritual. The word tantra actually means "woven together." The sexual aspects of tantra are focused on expanding intimacy and creating connected, even magical experiences, with or without genital penetration. Margot Anand is one of the world's leading authorities on tantra and best-selling author of *The Art of Sexual Magic*. She writes about the potential for generating sexual energy as fuel for manifesting what you desire. "In the heat of passion, in the depths of orgasmic pleasure," she writes, "normal ways of thinking and behaving change dramatically [. . .] Through deep sexual union, you can feel oneness not only with your beloved, but with all things. You can feel harmony with the whole cosmos, you can fall in tune with the eternal dance of existence." (Anand 1996).

These days, there are all kinds of tantric approaches to explore, ranging from ancient to modern style practices. All of these reveal cosmic aspects through guiding us to slow down and explore the fullness of the moment—with awareness, breath, energy, and touch. A fundamental aspect of tantra is syncing breath with your partner. It turns out breathing together is a shockingly simple way to create an energetic bond that takes us beyond everyday gripes and frustrations to an expanded consciousness. The beauty of this is that whether we feel a strong desire for sex or not, we can bond and boost our energy with a partner. At times, this energy even generates feelings of attraction. Breathing together is powerful when couples have a negative interaction and want to reconnect, and when they need it, a jump start to their sexual vitality. It is also a simple and powerful doorway for those who want more depth.

Tantra also includes powerful healing practices to release sexual trauma and shame, including massage for the yoni—the Sanskrit word for vulva—and lingam—the Sanskrit word for penis. At first, this may seem bizarre, but this practice helps clear past baggage and experiences that restrict our capacity to give and receive love, which inevitably dulls connection and sexual satisfaction. During these massages, the partner who gives the massage brings loving touch and attention to the others' genitals. The receivers allow themselves to express whatever sensations and emotions arise, from pleasure and lightness to fear and anger. The purpose is not to "get off" but to allow memories and stuck energy that is stored in the body to release. Sometimes the practice is orgasmic and other times not. After releasing tension, people report feeling freer and more able to enjoy sex and intimacy.

To explore a more soulful, tantric kind of sex, we do not have to start with performing ancient rituals. We can begin by simply becoming more mindful. Rather than rushing into sex, we can slow down and become present to ourselves and a partner. Taking a few breaths to recognize and cherish the connection with a partner and to be more intentional can create a much more intimate experience. Instead of following an agenda, we can check in with each other through words and touch. This allows what is exciting and alive to arise, moment to moment, in an intimate way. Sex has a better chance of being fresh, rather than habitual.

KAREZZA

In her book *Cupid's Poisoned Arrow: From Habit to Harmony in Sexual Relationships*, Marnia Robinson writes about her experience with a sexual practice called the Karezza method. The word comes from the Italian word "caress" and was first coined in America by Dr. Alice Bunker Stockham, a Chicago obstetrician and feminist. Caress is a fitting theme for the practice because it is about connecting sexually in a gentle way and letting go of the goal of orgasm. It is not about avoiding orgasm per se, but about being as relaxed as possible with sexual energy, rather than making orgasm the goal. The gentleness helps partners stay present and learn to attune to each other. (Robinson, 2010)

Robinson writes that orgasm, while pleasurable in the moment, can cause everything from disconnection to disgust between partners after the fact. In talking with thousands of people about sex, I discovered that some people feel post-sex blues. After the high of an orgasm, they can become sad or depressed. Other people feel a lack of interest in sex, or their partner, after a sexual experience. This is commonly portrayed in movies with men rolling over and falling asleep after sex. Movies do not show the aftermath of this dulled energy, however, which can last much longer than one night. "The subconscious cascade of neurochemical events appears to take a full two weeks to return to homeostasis," Robinson writes. She describes this as "cupid's poison" because, while sex is seen as a way to create a more loving and bonded feeling, the opposite can actually happen.

Due to a refractory period—the time after orgasm in which our chemical balance makes us less psychologically or physically interested in climaxing again—sex creates a fluctuation between desire and aversion. Aversion can become more frequent than desire. In the first year they shifted their sex to the Karezza style, Robinson reports that her lack of desire shifted to a more lighthearted and connected feeling. She and her husband became excited to touch each other more regularly.

When orgasm is the goal of sex, people can feel alone in the midst of a shared experience. As we become more aware, we can feel when a partner is tuned out or focusing only on their own pleasure. Karezza sex guides couples to have gentler and less frenetic sex by encouraging partners to relax their bodies as energy builds, rather than the common response of tensing the body as energy builds. The relaxation can create a smooth and nourishing energetic flow through the body and for the couple.

Karezza is a great option that allows a partner with a slower or lower sex drive to warm up and feel less pressure to be immediately turned on. It also creates less pressure for either partner to orgasm. Couples can avoid the ups and downs of the neurochemical dips in the refractory period that cause aversion and sporadic desire. Some degree of mismatched sex drives is common for couples to experience, and Karezza can be a bridge for couples to come closer more often, rather than drift apart.

ORGASM PAIRED WITH MEDITATION

Dr. Laurie Mintz, author of the book *Becoming Cliterate: Why Orgasm Equality Matters—And How to Get It,* coined a phrase called the Orgasm Gap. She writes that women in heterosexual relationships are having fewer orgasms than men. This can cause women to feel a range of emotions, from anxious because their bodies are not cooperating, to angry because their partners may not care or pay enough attention to their orgasm. (Mintz, 2017)

As we expand sex beyond genital penetration, we discover a wider range of ways to touch that can lead to orgasm. A powerful practice for exploring sexual energy and sensation is called stroking. This was created by the Morehouse community in California in 1968 and often focuses on women's clitoral orgasms, but it can include orgasm for people of all genders.

A few other names have been given to this practice over the years: Deliberate Orgasm (DOing), and Orgasmic Meditation (OMing) to name a few. Whatever we call it, the practice is an intentional way to explore sexual energy without genital penetration. Similar to tantric massage, the practice involves a giver and a receiver.

The receiver is undressed, at least from the waist down. The giver sits next to the receiver, using their finger to stroke the clitoris, the head of the penis, or another exquisitely sensitive body part. The experience is generally timed to last for fifteen minutes.

With the stroking practice, there is potential for pleasure or even a climax to happen. But, similar to Karezza, letting go of the goal of orgasm allows participants to open to a sensational ride. Rather than ending in an orgasm that has a high peak, followed by a sharp drop, sensations continue to build and flow through the body. The giver supports this by attuning to the receiver and learning to intuit the kind of touch, pressure, and speed that keeps the receiver in a state of pleasure without "going over the edge"—having a peak climax that releases energy and sensation like a typical orgasm does. This skill takes time to cultivate, to the point where the giver can intentionally bring the receiver's energy up and down, and end by creating a feeling of grounding, rather than dropping. Though the practice is usually time bound, to create a sense of safety and decrease pressure for both partners, it is possible to explore these waves of energy for long periods of time.

Many couples report feeling more balanced, connected, and turned on when they add this to their repertoire. I believe this is, in part, because of the mindfulness component, as well as the support to open to bigger energies. This allows one to relax, rather than tense up, in bed and in situations that are chaotic or surprising. Both partners become more familiar with presence and attuned attention, similar to states we can access through meditation. But unlike conventional meditation, integrating sensuality with it opens up pleasure pathways, which can range from gently loving to intensely passionate.

This experience is not only pleasurable for the receiver. The giver experiences pleasure as well by learning to feel the receiver's sensations in their own body. As we expand our capacity to feel our partner's sensations in our own body, pleasure becomes exponential! As a result, the giver and receiver can also feel a sense of merging, as though they are one body.

A PLEASURE PORTAL

These are three great options to begin to expand sex beyond the limited, culturally prescribed norms many of us get stuck in. They will inevitably feel awkward at times, especially in the beginning. But we can be honest about the awkwardness with our partners, rather than hide it. The more honest we are, the more connected we become. In the next chapter, we will explore an expanded sense of what orgasm actually is to allow for even more pleasure and connection.

One more cornerstone is imperative for a satisfying sex life: understanding our own anatomy. Only when we are familiar with our own bodies and turn-ons can we have a truly satisfying sex life. For many of us, our genitals, and our whole body as an erogenous zone, are unexplored territories. If we don't know how our body works, what we long for, and what excites us, we cannot tell someone else how we want to be held, touched, or loved. Inviting someone into our own knowing of our body and desires is one of the greatest portals to intimacy and more expansive sex.

Regena Thomashauer (also known as Mama Gena) is the author of many books, including *Pussy: A Reclamation*. She is also the creator of the School of Womanly Arts, a series of classes that focuses on supporting women to celebrate their sensuality and feel more empowered and inspired in all areas of their lives. She has taught tens of thousands of women to get to know their bodies and their emotions—what turns them on and how they like to be touched and cherished. When I participated in her Pleasure Boot Camp, she used a hand puppet in the shape of a vulva to describe the anatomy in a loving, informative way. She also showed us images of women's vulvas, of all shapes and sizes, to free women from the shame we often have about whether our size or shape is somehow flawed. Then she gave the assignment for women to explore their own vulvas at home, noting everything from color to texture and scent. Everything, she says, should be celebrated.

While I don't know of any all-male workshops where men explore their sexual organs in this fashion, there are tantra and sex education workshops with body and genital exploration, including the Human Awareness Institute (HAI) and the Body Electric School. HAI has a mission to promote personal growth and social change by replacing ignorance, shame, and fear with awareness, acceptance, and love. Their workshops also foster consensual, nourishing sexuality. The Body Electric school runs educational workshops to integrate the erotic with the sacred.

No matter how or whether you decide to explore, transforming the shame we feel about our bodies is very healing. It opens the doorway to more love, acceptance, and pleasure. And not only does transforming shame improve our intimate relationships, it boosts confidence and satisfaction in all areas of life!

PRACTICE

People who do not limit themselves to genital touch or strive for orgasm experience more pleasure more often. Imagine what your sex life would be like as you expand your definition of how sex can happen. With practice, you can heighten your capacity to feel more subtle sensations. Sexual pleasure can happen from being touched anywhere on your body or even without being physically touched. You can become more aware of and permeable to another's energy, expanding the pleasure you feel by feeling their pleasure too.

To explore your ideal sex life, let's first explore the beliefs that limit your sexual satisfaction. Many of us grew up hearing that aspects of sex are dirty or perverted, and people who enjoy sex are somehow deviant. Others never heard anything about sex, so their ideas about it were formed in isolation. No matter what beliefs are limiting you, the more clearly you see them, the more freedom you can get from them.

Make a list of your limiting beliefs about sex—the ideas that create restriction or fear, rather than allowing for delight or excitement. You may have heard the ideas from the media, caretakers, teachers, family members, or peers. As you list them, you may be surprised to discover beliefs you did not know were there. Sometimes, it's not until we inquire that we find what has been unconsciously impacting us. Complete this sentence to make your list:

The beliefs that keep me from wanting or enjoying sex as much as I want to are:

Examples:

Good girls don't like sex

Having thoughts about sex is perverted and dirty

I am only supposed to feel pleasure if someone else is feeling it too

Write your own . . .

Now that you have revealed some of the beliefs that keep you from having the sex life you want, make a list that describes what you want more of in your sex life. You may want more physical sensation—anything from pleasure to pain. You may want more emotional connection—to feel cherished, loved, or understood. You may want to play with power—being in or out of control.

Take some time to imagine what would feel pleasurable, meaningful, and connecting. Notice if you get caught wondering whether something is possible. If so, write it down anyway. The first step is to open the doorway to your desires. This builds on Chapter 4's prompt to list experiences you would want if you asked for 100 percent of your desires. Complete this sentence to make your list:

My vision of an expanded sex life would include:

Examples:

I feel intimately connected with my partner before and during sex

I speak up when pleasure fades or I feel uncomfortable

I allow the part of me that wants to play with domination and surrender to ask for this

Write your own . . .

_____

_____

Remember that when you feel stuck, it is a great time to get some help. Many of us had challenging or traumatic experiences in our youth and formative romantic relationships. These can keep our imaginations limited. I find the wisdom of Emily Nagoski helpful here. Nagoski, author of *Come as You Are: The Surprising Science That Will Transform Your Sex Life*, reminds us that it is important to keep pleasure at the heart of how we define sex.

"When you put pleasure at the center of your definition of sexual well-being," Nagoski says, "everything changes. When you let the desire emerge in response to pleasure, all the puzzle pieces of your sexuality come together in a brand-new way." As you explore what an expanded sex life would be, remember there is no wrong way to do this. As Nagoski says, "If you are experiencing pleasure, you are doing it right." (Darozhkina, 2018)

CHAPTER 7

WHAT IS ORGASM HONESTLY?

————

A male client in his late thirties came to me struggling to know if he was attracted to a woman he had started to date. He thought he was, but he said his body was telling him otherwise because he was not getting as aroused as he had with women in the past. We explored this situation, making it safe to hear what his body was attempting to communicate to him. As we peeled back the layers, we found his fear of being rejected by this woman. He was shocked to discover the fear was arising because she seemed like a great partner for him, which made him feel vulnerable. He realized he needed more of an emotional connection with her to feel safe to open his body! He was nervous to ask for it, but when he eventually did, he found that his turn-on came back.

Coaching people through relationships in their twenties through sixties has given me innumerable opportunities to talk about sex throughout various stages of people's lives. Many of the conversations with people as they age involve an inquiry into why sex is less exciting than in their youth. From a cultural perspective, many of us are sold the idea that passion fizzles over time in long-term relationships. From my experience, this is a sadly uneducated view of sex and orgasm. When people tell me sex is less exciting than it used to be, I know the door to expanded sex and orgasm has not been discovered. Otherwise, they would be experiencing richer, more connected, passionate sex and orgasms than they ever had before.

I have had male partners who, once they had an orgasm, decided our sexual experience was over. I have also had male partners who made a point to explore the terrain of expanded and multi-orgasmic pleasure. It does not take much to imagine which is more fulfilling. The difference between the quick burst of pleasure an average-length orgasm provides—around ten to fifty one seconds—and the hours of pleasure that are possible when we shift to exploring expanded orgasm is astonishing. Through exploring tantra and orgasmic meditation techniques, I have had experiences that are difficult to find words to explain. I don't know who is to blame for so many people not knowing how expansive orgasm can be, but it is time you know the whole truth. Many people never learn there is a wide range of intimacy and orgasm you can access.

WHAT IS ORGASM HONESTLY?

Orgasm is commonly referred to as a time during which a person experiences peak pleasure in a sexual experience, followed by a decrease in sexual tension. Most definitions describe the physical contractions that take place in the genitals, accompanied by ejaculation for males. When describing orgasm, physiological changes are emphasized by medical professionals, while the emotional and cognitive reactions are what psychologists and mental health professionals focus on. A single, integrated explanation of orgasm does not seem to exist.

A few models expound a bit on blood vessel dilation and involuntary muscular contractions, but, as with the definition of sex, I am disappointed to find these framings missing the mark on many levels. Ejaculation does not have to accompany orgasm in men, and women can also ejaculate with orgasm. Pleasure does not have to be limited to the genitals, and whole-body orgasms are not mentioned anywhere. Energy can move through the body, initiating pleasurable and energetic openings in the heart and head. Energy expansion can create powerful, transcendent experiences too. While the typical definition is limited, the benefits of orgasm are not. Many people experience better moods, increased productivity, and relief from daily anxieties and concerns. For many people, orgasm is a good thing, so let's explore how to make them more powerful and more likely!

Susan Bratton, who calls herself an "Orgasmanaut," joined me on the *Man Alive* podcast for Episode 112, "More Pleasure for Men." Bratton describes how orgasm is much more wide-ranging than many of us imagine. "I have gone to the furthest outreaches of orgasm, studying cumming, and cumming in as many ways as I could, for as long as I could, as hard as I could for a decade, to figure it out!" she told me. *That's a fun way to do research!* (Bratton, 2019)

Bratton describes fourteen different types of orgasms, including heartgasms and Godgasms. Although these may sound strange, I will never forget the first time I felt my heart burst open during a sexual experience. It was like having a genital orgasm but in my heart. A flood of energy and light opened in my chest. I realized then that sexual energy is simply energy. It can be felt *everywhere* in our bodies. For those who enjoy tapping into the energetic realms of sex, this energy extends beyond the body too, perhaps even opening us up to connect with our souls. We only have to become aware of our potential for these expanded states to become available to everyone. It takes some practice, but it is not a bad way to spend time, and this can supercharge your physical and spiritual energy.

Spiritual teachings prove that our energy fields extend beyond our bodies. We are more permeable and connected than many of us realize. This means that in addition to expanding beyond our bodies, we can expand to feel others' pleasure and orgasm too. Connecting with others when we are in permeable and transcendent states is what sexual tantra and other ancient orgasmic practices focus on.

ANCIENT ORGASMIC ROOTS
Orgasmic practices have existed for thousands of years and have roots in Taoism. Mantak Chia, one of the most well-known Taoist teachers, has written dozens of books, including *Cultivating Female Sexual Energy* and *The Multi-Orgasmic Man*. He translated the principles of Taoist sexual practice into more accessible terms for Westerners.

Since Chia's teachings integrate sexual energy with the physical, mental, and spiritual energy bodies, he talks about how sex and orgasm "[develop] human life energy—qi—for self-healing and life transformation." In Taoist orgasmic practices then, it makes sense that orgasm is much more than a burst of physical pleasure or release. It is a doorway to our life force, a way to move healing energy throughout our bodies, and a pathway to access deeper states of consciousness. Orgasmic energy can be like an emotional Roto-Rooter, clearing out the shame and wounds we hold in our bodies. This opens us up to healthier, more pleasurable living. (Chia, 2009)

When Chia's orgasmic practices came to the West, Drs. Victor and Suzanne Baranco coined the term Deliberate Orgasm, or Doing, as explained in Chapter 6. The Barancos' experiment in pleasurable group living has lasted for more than fifty years as a community called Morehouse in Lafayette, California. The Barancos felt that for a group to live together cohesively and with longevity, sensuality needed to be a part of the equation. (Morehouse, 2022)

They believed one of the components of pleasurable living was female equality and pioneered the importance of the clitoris in female orgasm in the 1960s and 1970s. This brought the equality of orgasm for women to the forefront. While many men do not objectify women sexually, many women have experienced their orgasm as a lower priority, or more complex and unreachable, during sex. As we explore equitable, honest, and vulnerable relationships, it becomes easier to let go of striving for ten-second orgasms and explore higher-caliber orgasms instead!

FAST-FOOD VERSUS FIVE-STAR CLIMAX

As I studied tantra and orgasmic practices like Morehouse's stroking and its subsequent forms, there were times when I felt angry that I had missed out on so much potential pleasure. I was grateful to finally experience moments when shame, anxiety, and self-consciousness faded away and what was left felt like pure love. I also mourned the time I had lost as a result of never hearing anyone talk about pleasure or transcendence that reaches a soul level. Some of my freedom moments were in the midst of sexual experiences, but others happened when I simply gazed into someone's eyes and felt met or seen without any genital contact.

The way I learned there was more possible with orgasm than I previously knew was comical. I was washing my hands in the bathroom at a personal growth workshop. The woman next to me was glowing. I said so, and she shared that she attributed it to her participation in another workshop where she was studying expanded orgasm. Most people are not fortunate enough to have a random bathroom conversation lead to a lifetime of better orgasms.

What I discovered is that orgasms (for those who have normative sexual experiences), are akin to eating fast food, rather than enjoying the fare at a Michelin-rated, five-star restaurant. I would not call typical orgasms bad, but they are a one-dimensional experience, composed of physical sensations of pleasure. Expanded orgasms are more of a three- or four-dimensional experience. We feel not just our physical sensations, but our emotional and energetic ones too. On top of that, we can feel our partners' experiences in all of these dimensions. This can be hard to digest for those who, up until now, have only dined on fast food or had one-dimensional orgasms. But I promise it is never too late to experience a wider range of pleasure, connection, and human potential.

Honesty is an important foundation of the five-star, multidimensional orgasm because expanding orgasm does not start with physicality. Instead, we have to learn to be more present, self-aware, and communicative. Mindfulness and meditation are great places to start tuning in, slowing down, and paying more attention. Our senses then become heightened, and we can be aware of subtleties. Then we can learn to attune to these subtleties in ourselves and others.

Rather than overlooking, or simply moving on, when someone's skin flushes in the heat of the moment, for example, we can start to feel *their* heat in *our* body. This increases our pleasure in an exponential way. We can begin to notice and viscerally feel our partner's muscles tensing or relaxing, their heart opening or closing, and these clues allow us to alter our responses. We can make choices to build energy and connection, rather than lose it. We can learn to stay in sync and expand, rather than get stuck in rote or prescribed sexual experiences.

Honesty is also crucial because in order to know what we need or want, like, or dislike, we have to be honest with ourselves. Instead of disassociating, getting distracted, or veering off into experiences of being "alone together," honesty keeps us connected with a partner. Honesty and vulnerability create more intimacy and pleasure than new techniques or positions ever could! Telling a partner what we notice, in ourselves and in them, is like a dance. Orgasms become more likely as partners attune to each other in this way. And as we learn to feel the rise and fall of our partner's energy in our own body, it can feel like merging—like we have four arms, four legs, two torsos, and all the genitals. Orgasm is then not only more likely to happen, it expands to the four-dimensional type.

My clients' experiences prove that the foundation of great sex and orgasm is far beyond the physical. When clients talk to me about sex, 90 percent of our conversations are about emotional and relational dynamics. When these dynamics are clear and connected, we do not need fancy skills or new positions to make sex and orgasms amazing. As we unpack frustrations, the underlying layers are most often caused by a lack of connection or collaboration. Getting honest about everything from insecurities and fears to desires and moment-to-moment blocks to connection allows our bodies to relax into pleasure in a way that makes orgasm much more likely.

ORGASM TO BUILD RATHER THAN KILL ATTRACTION
The typical peak and drop orgasms that most people have are great, but they can create dips in our neurochemistry. The Karezza method I described in Chapter 6 is one way around the hormonal and relational dip that happens in the refractory period when dopamine levels drop. Dopamine is one of the neurohormones that drops, which can then cause depression, anxiety, and lack of energy and ambition. When this is repeated on a regular basis, couples can be on a roller-coaster ride of attraction, not realizing attraction and passion could remain steadier. (Robinson, 2010)

Less familiar is the type of orgasms that keep sexual energy, attraction, and intimacy between partners alive and buzzing. These more expanded types of orgasm, that I began to describe in Chapter 6, are what Alicia Davon, relationship coach and co-facilitator of the Pleasure Course, teaches her students. Davon, a colleague, and friend of mine for decades, told me in an interview that most people think of orgasm as "a climax involving a very high peak and then a very sharp drop off in sensation, but a meditative orgasm lasts for minutes or even hours." This type of orgasm helps couples avoid the refractory period and is experienced as "rolling hills of sensation rather than a mountain peak with a drop," says Davon.

Davon has spent the past twenty years teaching about orgasm and even doing extended orgasm demonstrations where people can watch—yes, watch her orgasm!—and learn how to access these heightened states. She agrees that the "heightened pleasure, bliss, and mindlessness is not only for the one receiving the touch, but for the one giving it as well." This fits with my experience. The one who is touching or giving the orgasm is not just working hard without personal benefit. They can experience a kind of trance state, feeling and merging with the receiver's sensations. The state of expanded orgasm opens up a realm of merging and connection that takes intimacy to a whole new level. Partners who experience this have told me it deepens their capacity not only for pleasure, but to trust each other and be in sync in their daily lives.

An orgasmic demonstration may be wild to imagine, but it has great potential to dissolve sexual fear and taboo. Many of my clients were shamed in their youth for talking about, wanting, or experimenting with sex. A great sex life is hard to have if we do not have a place where sexuality, relationship, and intimacy can be discussed openly. While exploring orgasm in public may not be for everyone, we can always do this, or other practices, in the privacy of our homes.

When Alicia and her partner do a demo, they guide people to meditate beforehand, to become more permeable to Alicia's sensations. This shows us that not only can we feel our own and our partner's sensations, but we can tap into and feel the sensations of other people and places. The environments we move through, the food we eat, the art we see, and the people we talk to all become fodder for opening up our body and increasing our energy. When we pay closer attention, everything we experience piques at least one of our five senses. As we focus on *feeling* these sensations, rather than just *thinking* about them, we feel more sensation and pleasure in our bodies. The more we focus on the subtleties of those sensations, the more orgasmic we become. Feeling, rather than thinking, about our experience is a way to add dimension to the pleasure and connection we feel.

My clients often come to me feeling as though their worth is tied to their ability to have or give an orgasm. This is heartbreaking because it takes the fun and pleasure out of sex and cuts off the intimacy that occurs when the focus is on enjoyment, rather than accomplishment. "Extended orgasm," Davon says, "is a state of pleasure with high levels of arousal, but the body remains relaxed." Instead of tensing as sensation builds, as many people do as orgasm nears, we can relax our bodies. This builds pleasure that rises to greater heights and can fill every inch of our bodies, rather than just our genitals.

This amount of pleasure and intimacy tends to create an upward spiral in intimacy that allows relationship tensions to decrease. Davon laughed as she told me about the personal benefits of a regular orgasmic practice in her relationship. "When my partner, Erwan, creates that kind of pleasure with me, the little annoyances—like when he gets grouchy or irritable or bossy—roll off my back and just go away." The orgasmic practice then not only leads to more pleasure, but can cut down on the upsets couples experience. Many couples tell me they bicker less when having cuddle sessions or sex regularly. Consciously integrating orgasm into our lives (with or without intercourse) supports a more balanced nervous system and fewer fights and disagreements.

ORGASMIC LIFESTYLE

While most clients who come to me had not previously thought to pair meditation or mindfulness with orgasm, this paradigm shift is life changing. As I explored meditative orgasm, in addition to expanding pleasure, it brought more energy, excitement, and confidence to other areas of my life. Why? As Chia describes, orgasmic energy is not contained in intercourse or sexual experiences. Sexual energy is qi—*the vital energy that animates the body internally.* As the vital energy flows, both our orgasms and our lives become more energized.

There are people who take the concept of orgasm to the next level and talk about an orgasmic lifestyle. The focus here is on orgasm not just being a sexual climax, but a way to relate with life. It is about engaging our senses and opening up to more pleasure in our daily experiences. In my studies, I discovered we have the capacity to walk around with pleasurable, expansive energy flowing through us. We can shift from feeling dull or drained by focusing on our sensations and our surroundings.

This makes walking down the street, eating dinner, having a conversation, and even mundane tasks feel more enlivening.

I remember sitting at a restaurant on a break from one of my expansive orgasm workshops in San Francisco. The assignment over dinner was to feel the energy of what was happening around us in our bodies. I looked up at a neon sign and instead of simply seeing it, I felt its energy. The lights and colors swirled inside me as physical sensations. Since then, I have continued to explore how temperatures, textures, lights, and sounds can evoke an increase of energy in our bodies, which improves our physical, mental, and emotional states.

An orgasmic lifestyle is one where we pay attention to our life energy. We prioritize what makes us feel vital, rather than what dulls our energy. We experience life through all of our senses, rather than just thinking about life. Living this way increases the energy we have for our loved ones and has a positive impact on the world. With all of the stresses and complexities of modern-day life, prioritizing our qi could actually save us from the anxiety, depression, and mental health issues that so many of us experience.

PRACTICE

To increase your likelihood to have expanded orgasms, it is important to uncover any limited views of orgasm you have and anything that could keep you from experiencing a wider range of sensation and pleasure. Here are some great explorations to journal or talk about with a friend or partner.

What were your ideas about orgasm before reading this chapter?

_____

_____

_____

_____

_____

_____

_____

What limitations did your previous thoughts create for you in your orgasms?

_____

_____

_____

_____

How would you like to expand your orgasms? What might get in the way?

What is the first step you would like to explore to expand your orgasms?

_____

_____

_____

_____

_____

_____

_____

_____

_____

Answering these questions will help you get to know yourself better and will help others understand you better. You can also choose to build on this by exploring expansive orgasm practices. I suggest beginning with the experiment of letting go of striving to reach an orgasm. This does not mean an orgasm will not happen, but you can play with shifting your goal from the tension-oriented, peak-and-drop orgasm to allow energy to build and move through you. You may then experience the rolling-hills type of climax Davon talked about, which lasts much longer than a typical orgasm.

You can do this on your own or with a partner. While your orgasm may or may not expand the first time you try this, the most important part here is to make everything that happens right, rather than wrong. Build on the pleasure you experience and let go of trying to get this right! Remember that the foundation of a great orgasm is emotional and relational, so this is not just about finding a new template for a physical experience. Allow yourself to flow with the energy and pleasure and open up to feeling more subtleties in yourself or with a partner.

Here are a few more options for exploration. You can:

- Play with feeling your partner's sensations in your own body. As you witness changes in their energy or state, check in to see what you feel in your body.

- Focus on staying relaxed and unclenching your body in the midst of a sexual experience.

- Imagine the energy that builds in your genitals moving up your spine or to your heart or head. You can also practice sensing—or imagining—it circulating up your back and down the front of your body in an energetic loop. If you are with a partner, you can connect these energy circuits between your bodies too; this is a central tantric technique.

- Explore how much pleasure you can allow yourself to feel in body parts other than your genitals. This is the foundation for the whole-body orgasm.

Be kind to yourself as you explore new ways of opening your heart and body. This is exciting, and it can also feel vulnerable. Since this book is not a how-to manual, you can reference the recommended resources at the end of the book if you are inspired to explore the practices I cover here.

CHAPTER 8

THE MYTH OF HAPPY SEX

———

My partner pulled his face away from mine with tenderness and a hint of sadness. "You're not into this, are you?" he asked. We were lying in bed. I was distracted as we kissed, drifting into thought rather than focusing on him. The red walls surrounding my bed normally seemed passionate and warm, but I was nearly numb.

Hearing his words, I paused and checked in to see what was going on. The first emotion I noticed was fear. I was afraid I would offend him, or he would be mad at me if I was not happy or excited. I did not want to set off a domino effect where we both felt bad and needed time to recover, killing our chance for intimacy. We had such limited time together as parents and business owners who only saw each other once a week.

As I reflected, I knew he was not the cause of my fear. It came from a lifetime of emotional dynamics, from past romantic relationships, formative relationships, and the cultural idea that happiness is more attractive than "darker" feelings like sadness, anger, or hurt. Knowing this helped, but there was still a layer of fear blocking me from seeing more truth. I was not yet being fully honest with myself.

Moments like these are pivotal for couples. When the fear of upsetting or hurting another shows up, it is common to feign happiness to appease the other. Someone may force a smile and say "I'm fine," carrying on to try to make the uncomfortable thing go away. Many couples create and eventually solidify a distance between them as a result. The distance often widens and dulls intimacy over months, years, and decades.

I knew avoiding honesty would not bring us closer, so I dug deeper to find what I was feeling beneath the fear. I found it. A few hours earlier I had attended a funeral. My heart was heavy. I did not realize before we got in bed that my heart was full of grief. But as soon as our intimacy opened my heart, the pain was unavoidable.

Instead of attempting to act happy, I was honest. I told him about my heavy heart. I cried. He kissed my tears and listened to me grieve. He was present and connected in a way I hear women long for in many relationship conversations. After I felt the grief, I could feel my body again. I went from being numb to feeling many sensations, including a softer heart and reignited attraction.

I did not try to appease him, and he did not try to get me to be happy. We both knew those strategies would cut off our connection. We were willing to endure the discomfort of honesty, rather than feign happiness. And it was the honesty that brought us back together and even re-ignited passion.

HAPPINESS IS NOT A PREREQUISITE

The belief that we should be happy, and that we are more attractive when we are, is passed down through cultural, religious, and family beliefs. Many clients tell me they were encouraged by their parents, siblings, or teachers to "get over it" when they were young and upset. In response, they learned to hide any feeling other than happiness. This pattern showing up in our sex lives is no surprise. My clients have revealed that attempting to be happy when they are not, or trying to get their partner to feel good, cuts off connection and keeps sex from being intimate, hot, or playful.

A common idea people bring to me is that if their partner is not happy, sex will not happen. However, it is much more complicated than this. While sex may be more likely to happen when people are feeling good, this does not account for the famed and steamy "make-up sex" that many people report as some of the hottest sex of their lives. The energy of upset and anger can ignite passion and arousal. As trust is built, vulnerability pairs with anger to create passionate intimacy.

In Laurie Handlers's book *Sex and Happiness: The Tantric Laws of Intimacy,* laws three, four, and five are focused on emotional release, honoring anger, and speaking our truth. It may be surprising that three of the ten laws in a book about sex and happiness focus on making room for emotions other than happiness. But she too recognizes the importance of couples getting honest, rather than "keeping the peace" or trying to stay happy. This also shows that what happens outside the bedroom has a powerful impact on what happens inside the bedroom. We cannot separate the two. (Handler, 2007)

In the midst of working on reigniting their sex life, a couple I coached was discussing a recent argument. The husband was supposed to pick up the dry cleaning by a certain time. The time passed, but he knew the cleaner's hours and planned to go before they closed. His wife was nervous because she needed her clothes the next day. When she could not get ahold of him, she went by herself, and he showed up a few minutes after she had left. The conversation that night was not pleasant. She was irritated because she felt she had to do it herself or it would not have happened. He was upset because he did not feel trusted. As we talked through the series of events, one of the most painful parts for her was when he said, "Can't we just forget about this and move on?"

The ability to move on after a disagreement is important. Moving on without mutual understanding, however, is a form of trying to get back to happy. It is a fleeting version of happiness, though—akin to shoving garbage under a cabinet, wondering why the room stinks, and avoiding the room, even though it used to be a lovely place to hang out. People close their hearts to avoid feeling their pain, not realizing their hearts close to each other too. Avoidance causes disconnection and mistrust to fester.

I knew this couple was running the risk of killing their sex life and their loving connection if they moved on without feeling understood. I gave each of them a chance to be heard. She first recognized that she was trying to be in control. When she teared up and vulnerably admitted she was struggling to feel supported, the air softened between them. Although it was not easy for him to hear, it was more effective than nagging or attempting to gain control.

He recognized that blowing off their agreed timeline was also an attempt to have control and freedom. His vulnerable admission was that he really wanted her to trust him, not just with the laundry, but with her heart. He was feeling lonely and unmet emotionally. These admissions, while challenging to share, brought them closer. They were the underlying layers that, when addressed, are more effective at resolving conflict than the surface layers. In these layers, we found the cause of the lack of trust on both sides and explored how each could feel supported and connected. Until that happened, passion was not likely to happen either.

Instead of trying to get back to happy, couples can prioritize getting to understanding. At times, it can seem like heading in an undesired direction away from sexiness. But staying curious and loving reveals new doorways to connection. This keeps passion from fizzling and can even reignite it.

COULD THE DESIRE TO GET BACK TO HAPPY BE KILLING YOUR SEX LIFE?

There are people who describe happiness as an emotion that comes and goes. Others see it as a state of mind—something that lasts longer and includes the ups and downs of a variety of emotions over a period of time. Sam Wren Lewis, author of *The Happiness Problem*, has an interesting view. "We can see happiness as an ongoing process of discovering what really matters," he writes. (Lewis, 2019)

From Wren's perspective, happiness is more complex than a passing emotion. It is intimately tied to our values and calls for ongoing discovery. I find that when this discovery is collaborative between partners, the bond becomes unshakable. Self-revealing, exploratory honesty is one of the most powerful ways I've found to create long-lasting connection and happiness beyond a passing moment.

When we only accept a happy version of ourselves or our partners, we cut off the intimacy that is the foundation of a thriving, evolving sex life. When we think happiness needs to precede sex, intimacy also fades. This has puzzled my clients who were taught that sex and sensuality should be happy. It should open us up to happiness and love. However, it is common that when we start to drop our guard and open our hearts, we feel anything we had been avoiding. After the funeral, I had unknowingly numbed myself to avoid the pain. But my strategy broke down when my partner acted lovingly toward me. Then, what was beneath the surface was revealed to us.

Many couples go farther into disconnection in moments of upset or distance. Panic can arise when stuck-ness, apathy, or an emotion that sidetracks sex comes up. If we are short on time, we may think "but if not now, then when will we have sex?" This can lead to pressuring ourselves or our partners to ignore our honesty and instead press on. We either override to move forward or go our separate ways in defeat. Knowing how to create connection in these vulnerable times gives another option: to deepen intimacy.

This starts with a perspective shift that turns irritation, apathy, and upset into a pathway to passion and connection. Instead of distraction or upset being a wall, it can be a doorway.

We can courageously get curious, rather than defending, attacking, or running away. When we explore and get curious together, an expanded version of sex starts to happen. Through riding waves of challenging emotions and differences, we reignite sparks and build trust.

Since avoiding our pain cuts us off from pleasure and aliveness, we have to make a different choice if we want to be intimate. Including a variety of moods and emotions makes our sex lives hotter, more meaningful, and more sacred. When we are accepted for who we are, especially in these vulnerable moments, growth and healing happen. Partners learn to explore sex that opens each other's hearts, releases pain, and evokes new levels of relaxation and pleasure. Welcoming emotions other than happiness paradoxically leads to connection that creates more happiness in the long term.

In my example, I realized I did not have to get back to happy to have sex. This revelation was freeing and life changing. I now know I can be close with someone no matter what moods we are in. We build trust and connection as we face the fear of being unlovable or undesirable. And although it is more vulnerable to show our hearts than to shut down or hide, the other option is to betray ourselves, which eventually causes a relationship to die.

When we no longer feel the need to pretend or put on a mask, true intimacy happens. As Jamie Wheal says, we can "show up on the mat" beyond moods or striving to get somewhere. We can connect and explore without a goal, rather than trying to preplan, reach a climax, or get back to happy.

IF YOU DON'T HAVE ANYTHING NICE TO SAY . . .

In my mid-twenties, I realized I was stuffing my anger and upset, attempting to be a "good, happy girl." I noticed I would hide my truth to try to keep the peace. But as a result, I would feel low or irritable, neither of which creates the freedom or aliveness needed for passion to ignite. Trying to be happy was creating resentment, cutting off intimacy, and killing my sex life.

Dr. Robert Glover, therapist and author of *No More Mr. Nice Guy*, asks the question: "Why do people try to change who they are?" In other words, why do we think we have to hide what we feel if it is something other than good? "After spending years examining Nice Guy Syndrome from every possible angle," Glover writes, "there is only one answer to this question that makes sense: because it does not feel acceptable for a boy or man to be who he is." (Glover, 2010)

This conundrum affects all genders. The struggle to feel okay being who we are and feeling what we feel is in some way true for every person I have met. In addition to her relationship coaching, Baczynski also created the Good Girl Recovery Program to support women with the socialization they receive to prioritize others' wants ahead of their own needs. Many people who identify as nice guys or good girls need help revealing their honesty, especially when upset or disappointed. Rather than believing a partner will stay and be supportive, they may shut down or pull away out of fear.

Growing up, I often heard, "if you don't have anything nice to say, don't say anything at all." This is an idea that caused me to feign happiness for a long time. I now see this statement as incomplete. Watching many clients struggle to ask for what they want or honestly reveal when they don't like something, I see the tendency to abandon ourselves in an effort to be nice.

Transforming this statement into one that actually helps couples create intimacy and passion would focus on us finding the underlying layers of our upsets and then revealing them with maturity, respect, and care. Instead of not saying anything at all, the new statement would be: "If you don't have anything nice to say, pause until you find something caring and mature to say." This helps us reorient from trying to save our relationships by being dishonest or feigning happiness. It allows us to stay true to ourselves and honest with our partners.

PRACTICE

Sex based on a passing mood of happiness eventually tends to become unsatisfying. You can enjoy more nourishing sex by starting to admit to feelings other than happiness. To be honest in a mature and connected way, you will have to understand the fears and motivations that cause you to hide or distract yourself. Take some time to answer the following questions. If you are single, you can do this on your own or with a friend. If you are in a romantic relationship, I suggest doing this together.

There are a couple structures that can work for this exercise. The first is to make a list. The second is to ask the questions out loud in a repeating format. You can take five to ten minutes for one person to ask while the other person answers and then switch roles. The person who asks simply says "thank you" after each response and asks again. There is no conversation during this, which will allow you to stay in the flow of your thoughts and feelings. If you want to share more, you can debrief after you have finished, which I highly recommend.

What am I afraid will happen if I admit my upsets, disappointments, or fears? *(For example, others will leave or think poorly of me.)*

_____

_____

_____

_____

_____

_____

_____

_____

What am I afraid will happen if my partner is not happy? *(For example, I will be a bad partner. It will be my fault if our relationship does not work.)*

_____

_____

_____

_____

_____

_____

_____

_____

What else is possible besides my fears? *(For example, it's possible my honesty could inspire us to be closer. I could feel more empowered.)*

_____

_____

_____

_____

_____

_____

_____

_____

_____

_____

What would make it safer for me to share honestly with those I care about? *(For example, if I knew they would listen, rather than defend themselves.)*

_____

_____

_____

_____

_____

_____

_____

When doing this with a partner, you can also ask questions to reveal dynamics that could be currently causing disconnection.

Do you feel judged, blamed, or misunderstood by me when you're not happy? What are some specific examples of what I do?

How can I support you when I notice you are not happy? In general and during sex?

_____

_____

_____

_____

_____

_____

_____

_____

_____

It may never be totally comfortable to reveal that we are not happy. I decided to commit to honesty over comfort after my divorce because comfort in the short term led me to dullness and resentment in the long term. Self-revealing honesty also does not have to feel like drudgery. In fact, it can feel uplifting, even when emotions are intense.

The Greeks had an expression for when truth is revealed and our hearts feel lighter as a result: Aletheia. They knew that even heavier emotions can feel freeing when we acknowledge and accept them, which one would expect from a culture that had mastered the art of drama.

If you watch children when they express emotions, you will see their emotions tend to come out big and loud. After a few minutes of releasing, however, they settle down. I have been shocked when my kid and I have a disagreement and five minutes later I am the only one still holding on to the upset. I can hold on to emotions for hours. There is a Buddhist idea that our emotions and thoughts are like clouds in the sky. Instead of jumping on the clouds and "riding them," we can allow them to pass by. When we recognize our emotions are transient, we stop letting them define us. This makes it easier to admit them to others and let go of the idea that we should be in a consistent state of happiness, in or out of the bedroom.

PART 3

CHAPTER 9

HOW TO IMPROVE RATHER THAN KILL YOUR SEX LIFE WITH HONEST CONVERSATIONS

―――

My mom handed me a cartoon book about sex called *Where Did I Come From?* when I was sixteen. She said she found it in her closet and meant to give it to me when I was eight. I found it last year and showed it to my kid, who was nine at the time and had no interest in the drawings of chubby, naked, middle-aged couples with genitals on full display!

For years, I was confused about why my parents had not talked about sex with me sooner. But now, as a mother, I get it. I hesitate to bring up the topic with my kid. Every time I try, I feel awkward. I don't know how much to say or when to instill an age-appropriate, inclusive, and inspiring understanding of sex. Do I bring it up in the car? Do I bring it up over dinner? How do we continue the conversation from when my kid was five, when I said the sperm and egg meet in "the canal?" We have moved on to an understanding that the "canal" is actually the vagina, but how much more detail do I share and when?

As I reread the cartoon book, I thought about the conversations I have about sex with my adult clients. I was struck by how the awkwardness of their conversations matched my awkward struggles to talk about sex with my kid. Many clients say they do not talk about sex with their partners because it is too uncomfortable and awkward. There never seems to be a good time. And they do not want to bring it up because they worry their partner will be upset, or worse, they might find out their partner does not like something they are doing in bed.

Most of us did not learn how to talk about sex, so it can feel scary and awkward to have these conversations. Experiences from youth often evoke shame that then creates avoidance or anxiety. I cannot count the number of people who come to me with versions of "I don't want to kill our sex life by talking about it." The irony is that the clients who are not talking about sex with their partner are not having great sex. So avoiding conversations about sex does not make sex better. Sometimes, talking about sex can be unsexy, especially when it is clinical or disrespectful, but talking about sex can also spark excitement and intrigue.

A client came to me and hesitantly brought up the fear that she might be "perverted." She had felt this way since she was five because of an innocent childhood moment where she and another kid looked at each other's genitals. In just a few minutes of talking about it, her fear released. She saw that the judgment she was holding about herself was her parents', not her own. We also found humor in the fact that being perverted as an adult does not have to be a bad thing, even though a part of her worried it was.

This client brought this memory to me because she feared rejection from her partner. It is such a shame that the fear of being rejected is stronger with people we love because it is incredibly healing to discuss our fears and desires with a supportive partner. Sometimes, it only takes a few minutes to shift old fears, like my client and I did in our session. The forty to seventy years it can take people to talk about their fears is what's heartbreaking because we miss out on so much healing and pleasure.

Revealing honesty takes courage, and it can be painful when it is not well received. Our fears can be worse than reality, though. Recently, another client told me about a date where he was vulnerable and honest. He told his date he would not hide himself. He said he had done it for too many years in a prior marriage and could no longer stand it. He risked rejection by telling her he felt vulnerable, and this was a time in his life when he did not have it all together. She was so touched by his honesty, she was moved to tears. She told him she trusted him more and was even more attracted to him as a result of his honesty and courage. This happens for many of my clients. They are often shocked to find that vulnerable honesty can be sexy.

FOUR FOUNDATIONS OF CONVERSATIONS ABOUT SEX THAT CREATE MORE PLEASURE AND CONNECTION

I teach my clients a few foundations of conversations to create the safety that allows for more pleasure, excitement, and connection. If both people do not feel safe to express their desires and concerns without being judged or shamed, these conversations go south quickly. Let's explore what makes these conversations welcoming, rather than awkward or altogether avoided.

1. PRIORITIZE CURIOSITY OVER FEAR AND DEFENSIVENESS

Fear is one of the biggest reasons our attention shifts from curiosity and exploration to defensiveness and judgment. When we feel afraid, we are prone to judge someone else's desire as strange or we focus on how it could be painful or disrespectful, rather than listening with curiosity. Instead of requesting a clearer understanding, we may pepper our partner with these fears, which can leave them feeling alone and attacked.

For example, if one partner reveals a desire to have sex more often, the other partner might bring up reasons why they are too busy or express resentment about how shouldering more of the shared responsibilities takes up their time. While these are valid concerns, this attitude shifts the conversation away from exploration. With a foundation of curiosity, the conversation would focus on gathering information, setting aside any decision about whether or not it will happen. We can ask questions like: "What excites you about this?" "If you had this, what would this do for you?" "Is there a number of times per week you are hoping for, or is it really more about the quality?" The person receiving the desire would gain understanding that allows for collaboration and negotiation based on the desire and the concerns that arise.

Hearing a partner's desire can feel vulnerable at times. A client once told me that when his partner shared a desire to try something new sexually, his first thought was, "Does she no longer find me sexy?" I hear similar self-doubts all the time. Even though a desire may have nothing to do with a partner's lack, people often wonder, "Am I letting my partner down sexually? Am I still wanted? Am I still attractive to this person?"

Curiosity is equally important when someone shares concerns about a desire. Clients tell me they have exploded or shut down when a partner asked questions about their desires. They felt cross-examined or made wrong. This could have to do with the questioner's style, but we can also unconsciously slip into defensiveness when giving more details about a desire feels vulnerable. Staying curious about a partner's concerns allows for collaboration.

Though challenging, especially at first, it is possible to explore desires and proposals without defensiveness or taking things personally. Hearing and exploring desires without grilling someone about their intentions or listing the potential downsides is possible. When we get curious and explore, we build trust and intimacy, rather than baggage and resentment.

2. GET TO THE ROOT OF A DESIRE

Getting to the root of a desire builds on curiosity by exploring underlying motivations. Often, when I ask my clients *why* they want an experience, it takes time to discover why it matters and how they would feel if it happened. They commonly say "I don't know. I just want it." As we stay with the question though, the reasons become clearer. Desires are multilayered—physical, emotional, relational, and even spiritual.

Take the example of someone wanting to experience being tied up. The act of being bound is the first layer of desire, but there are deeper motivations that vary by person. In this example, the deeper motivation for one person may be to have the physical sensation of being bound, whereas for another person the desire may be for the experience of being released from responsibility. For another person, the desire may be to fight and break free, and still another may relish the inability to do anything wrong because they are not free to act. Without understanding the deeper motivations, we cannot create experiences that meet a person's desires. We also run the risk of creating experiences that feel disrespectful or painful.

If someone wants their partner to wear lingerie, it could be the feel and look of lace or straps that are turn-ons, but for another, it may be more about a desire for new adventure. Understanding the deeper aspirations of a desire is incredibly helpful for couples because it expands the possibilities and flexibility of exploration. When an activity feels unsafe or scary to one partner, knowing the deeper motivations allows for collaborating to create other ways to experiment with the same desire. As couples start having conversations on this level, both their relationship and their sex life become more nuanced, interesting, and satisfying.

3. BE CLEAR WHETHER YOU ARE IN EXPLORING OR DECISION-MAKING MODE

Two people can be in the middle of the same conversation without realizing they are "not on the same page." One of the most common ways this happens is when one person is exploring possibilities and the other is attempting to make a decision. This has caused a lot of stress in both my business and romantic relationships.

I had a romantic partner who often wanted to talk about his desires with me. He felt closer when he voiced them out loud and said it was not always necessary to make them happen. These conversations were painful for me because I could not understand how someone could have a desire without needing to make it happen. I felt guilty when his desire did not match mine because I took these exploratory conversations to be decision-making conversations. I thought that if his desire went unmet, it would make me a bad partner. It took me years to realize that some desires can be fulfilling to explore without ever being acted out. Talking or fantasizing about them can ignite a spark.

Clarity about whether we are in an exploring or decision-making mode is priceless! When we clarify that we are in an exploratory conversation, it takes the pressure off of us to make something happen. It becomes easier to be curious because the goal is not to strategize or plan, but to understand each person's desires and concerns. Ideally, we learn about ourselves in the process and see how a desire could benefit each person. The safety created by knowing that nothing will happen until both partners get to a "yes" can allow fear and anxiety to dissipate. Then partners can shift to decision-making mode when they are ready.

4. BE WILLING TO COLLABORATE

Collaboration is key with couples, but it is not always easy because we all show up with different styles, desires, wounds, and fears. Revealing these can feel more vulnerable than we might expect. Curiosity continues to be key, whether bringing or responding to a desire.

When we bring a desire to someone and are met with judgment, disgust, or just plain "no," it can be defeating and disappointing. A partner who takes the position of a firm "no" in response to a desire and says things like "I would never do that" or "No, that's not me" cuts off the potential for a collaborative conversation.

Instead of expressing anger or offense when we do not like the proposal, we can get collaborative. Rather than defensively exploding or collapsing into unenthusiastically going along, we can start by asking curious questions to find out more. We always have the right to say "no," but asking and collaborating creates new possibilities while simultaneously creating intimacy.

As we become more collaborative, we shift from a binary yes or no to seeing desires as multifaceted. One aspect of a desire may be exciting, even as others are scary or off-putting. Asking questions to learn more specifics allows us to find parts that are intriguing. With our previous example, in which one partner wanted more sex, the other partner might be more willing if they knew it would include their favorite style of sex. Although more sex on its own might sound stressful, playing with how it would be a win-win for each person diffuses tension and increases pleasure. When we are willing to explore and collaborate, we shift from conversations that are based in fear to conversations that are creative and playful.

Rather than saying a blanket "no" to a request, we can also consider what would need to change to make the request feel safe and exciting. "Maybe" is a great start for a collaborative conversation, as is creating time-bound experiments, or baby steps, toward a bigger desire. With the request to be tied up, for example, couples could create a five-minute experiment where all clothes stay on and one partner has their wrists bound. Rather than rushing toward a desire, fearing it won't happen if it doesn't all happen now, we can bring a mature attitude where we take one step at a time. Collaborating may mean that things do not move forward as fast as we would like, but intimacy builds every step of the way and new possibilities arise.

If a partner is not being curious about our desires, rather than attacking them, we can share our desire to be understood. A powerful question to evoke this is: "Would you be willing to be curious with me, rather than jumping to conclusions?" The less defensive we are, the more willing they will be to collaborate.

Now that we have laid out these foundations, let's turn our attention to the timing we are working with. There is no right time to have these conversations, but there are times that work better than others to discuss different aspects of our sexual experiences. When we know which phase we are in and what is best addressed at that time, we are likely to have a conversation that creates more connection, rather than less. When we are willing to share the deeper layers of what we think and feel, including our fear and awkwardness, passion and pleasure become more likely.

THE THREE PHASES OF SEX AND WHICH CONVERSATIONS TO HAVE WHEN

Many clients ask me when the "right" time to talk about sex is. My answer is that there is no ideal time to talk about sex, and it is great to talk about sex many times! There are three phases of a sexual experience, during which different aspects are best addressed. Simply put, they are:

1. Before

2. During

3. After

Each phase allows for unique connection and revelations. Distinguishing these phases helps create more effective conversations.

BEFORE SEX

Before having sex with someone, and periodically before ongoing sexual experiences, it is helpful to explore each person's likes and dislikes. It may seem that we all want the same things from sex, but sex feels good to each of us for different reasons. For some, sex blows off steam and creates more relaxation. For others, sex is about experiencing pleasure or feeling intimate and loved. Still for others, sex can involve stepping into new roles that do not feel safe outside the bedroom. Many of us enjoy sex for all of these reasons at different times. Knowing ourselves and our partners makes it more likely to have a sex life where desires and needs are met. But people often avoid these conversations, instead hoping things will go well.

I suggest starting conversations about sex before and outside of a sexual experience. When we are not in the heat of the moment, people tend to feel freer to be honest. Talking about sex in the before phase is a great time to dream and get creative. We can share desires and fantasies. We can take the time to explore awkwardness and fear with compassion. By learning about each other, couples experience less awkwardness and more intimacy when sex eventually happens.

DURING SEX

As a sexual experience is happening, it is not necessarily a great time for lengthy, intellectual, or theoretical discussions. It is, however, a powerful time to express desires and discomforts as they arise. Many people are afraid that communicating in the midst of sex will kill the mood and their chance to have sex. But the clarity and intimacy created from doing so can make it hotter and more pleasurable.

One of the most effective tools I remind clients of is simple—asking their partners questions. Many clients tell me they think they should already know what their partner likes, so they don't ask and don't know. I have seen men, especially, judge themselves as weak or unmanly if they do not already know. But trying to read each other's minds does not tend to go well, unless you have studied tantra or other intimacy practices for decades and have learned the skill of attunement.

Some ways of communicating in the midst of a sexual experience are more effective than others. Alyssa Morin is a somatic sex educator and relationship guide who helps people be more sexually satisfied. In *Man Alive* podcast Episode 104, we talked about different ways of asking questions that create different impacts. "In the midst of a sexual situation," Morin says, "it is helpful to ask questions that keep a person focused on their body and sensations, rather than bringing them back to their thoughts." (Morin, 2019)

One example is the difference between asking, "What would you like me to do right now?" versus "Would you like me to X or Y?" When we ask someone an open-ended question about what they want, there is an endless array of possibilities. Sometimes the possibilities are exciting, but, in the heat of the moment, their mind may not be in a state to offer options. Choosing from a menu of presented options is easier.

We can also use physical demonstrations to accompany the question "Would you like me to X or Y?" while acting out two different examples to help a person stay focused on their body. This often makes decision-making easier. For example, "Do you want more pressure or less pressure?" "Do you like my nails or the tips of my fingers?" When we let go of the idea that words and questions kill the moment or stunt pleasure, we can turn up the heat by asking about and demonstrating what is exciting and enjoyable.

I have held back from speaking about my discomfort many times out of a fear of offending someone. A powerful tool I learned in one of Davon's workshops that has helped is nick-named the Appreciation Sandwich. Rather than blurting out a complaint or frustration, we can sandwich our request between two appreciations. For the first appreciation, we share something we are enjoying. If we do not like the way someone is touching us, for example, the appreciation could be as basic as "Thank you for having your attention on me." It is an exercise in patience and compassion to be able to find something we like in the midst of something that feels uncomfortable or painful. The middle of the sandwich is the request. For example, "Would you be willing to slow down your touch?" The last appreciation is about the change they made, or what feels good to us as a result. One example would be "I love feeling your fingers moving slowly on my skin." The second appreciation can also be as simple as a moan or a "Thank you!"

Remember that most tools we use feel awkward at first. They become more comfortable over time. What works best in the midst of a sexual experience is to bring our desires, rather than our complaints.

AFTER SEX

Hoping or assuming more sex will lead to better sex is not a great strategy. So, I suggest having post-sex conversations, which I call debriefs. Debriefing sexual experiences is one of the best ways I know to ensure that our sex lives get better over time.

Many people do not speak up when something is uncomfortable or even painful because the fear of hurting someone can be stronger than the potential for future pleasure and intimacy. But then we miss out on learning each other's preferences and turn-ons. Knowing this information is what makes sex hotter and more intimate.

Think about a baker who tries out a new cake recipe and asks for feedback. A taste tester finds the consistency odd but is afraid to say so. So the baker offers this strange consistency cake to customers without knowing it is less appealing. This could cost the baker their business! Holding back our truth is similar and has cost many couples their relationships. When we withhold feedback, sex can become rote, boring, or disappointing. But it does not have to be this way.

Most of us need help cultivating the courage to ask for what we want in the moment, during a sexual experience. The debrief is an easier time to discuss vulnerable topics that then allow us to co-create amazing future experiences. I give clients a few simple questions to reveal helpful information, and they tend to not hurt people's feelings. Each person can take a turn answering these questions. The questions I give clients are:

- What did you enjoy about our sex? *(This starts the conversation with the mindset of appreciation.)*

- What could make our sex even better in the future? *(This focuses on desires rather than complaints.)*

- Is there anything that feels vulnerable about our experience that you can tell me now, even if you didn't say it then? *(This is a broader question that makes room for topics not covered in the first two questions.)*

If a partner is resistant to talking about sex, it can be helpful to set a context for this conversation. One way I have suggested clients introduce these questions is: "I'd love to keep having better sex, where you and I both feel more pleasure and connection. Would you be willing to answer a few questions a relationship coach said would make that more likely?" With this framing, a partner may be more able to see that there is something in it for them, rather than this being an overly analytical exercise.

If you have a partner who is still unwilling to talk about this, you can try bringing a combination of compassionate curiosity with a request that they be willing to try this at least once. You can also check in to see why this is so uncomfortable for them and what would make it feel safe. Are they afraid of hearing your disappointment or afraid to be honest? If so, you can make an agreement to bring mature honesty, which is loving and supportive, rather than immature honesty, which can be critical and demeaning. If there is a history of unwillingness to open up about personal topics, this would be a good reason to get some help from a coach or counselor.

When concerns or shame arise in the debrief, it is powerful to take time to talk about them. Although it may be uncomfortable, it is worth it. Otherwise, these issues can pop up again, years down the road. At that point, someone has spent a long time suffering and feels hopeless or distraught when something could have been addressed and collaborated on. Getting honest sooner can save a relationship.

PRACTICE

Finding ways to talk about sex will deepen connection with a partner and bring more excitement and variety. You can use these four foundations to have conversations, both while dating and in long-term relationships. I suggest exploring one of these perspectives or actions that is new to you from this chapter this week. You might try using the debrief conversation template or exploring the following questions based on the four foundations. Each foundation provides a chance to explore your habits and desires.

1. Prioritize Curiosity over Fear and Defensiveness

    a. What fears cause you to become defensive, rather than remain curious with a partner? What are you most afraid of?

2. Get to the Root of a Desire

    a. Choose a desire you have and look deeper to discover *why* you want it.

3. Be Clear Whether You Are in Exploring or Decision-Making Mode

    a. Set up a conversation where you explicitly state which mode you are in. Afterward, discuss the impact that getting clear about the mode had on your conversation.

4. Be Willing to Collaborate

    a. Choose a desire and consider how you could get collaborative with it. Instead of demanding that someone play along or denying you have the desire, consider how to make it a win-win.

Communicate about which practice you are taking on and/or choose one together. As you continue to clarify your needs and find the courage to speak up when something does not feel great, your relationship can become safer and stronger.

CHAPTER 10

SIX FUNDAMENTALS OF DEEPER INTIMACY AND BETTER SEX

———

I am walking in the woods with my partner, and we are having a conversation to process some tension between us. He feels I have not been prioritizing our relationship and is giving me a detailed list of how many more times he has texted me than I have texted him in the past few months. I am about to scream because I feel infuriated, attacked, and discounted. I pause and take a deep breath. In that pause, I remember that beneath his robotic accounting is a hurting human.

I remind myself of my commitment not to speak until I can say something kind and constructive. My head is hot, my stomach has dropped to my feet, and my throat is full of cotton. But instead of lashing out, I slowly say, "I can tell you're feeling hurt and uncared for. I don't know the reality of the numbers, but I want to explore this so you don't have to feel this way." Admittedly, my teeth were a bit clenched, but as I let go of my defenses, I opened up to being curious about whether I had stopped prioritizing our relationship, and if so, why. I knew that avoiding defensiveness would help us reconnect, rather than creating a battle where we each tried to prove we were right.

As I allowed for more vulnerability, I saw how complex human relationships are. We can feel close to someone one minute and distant the next. The more intimate a relationship, the more it can be like walking through a minefield, every step presenting a risk of explosion. Although neither party placed the land mines, there are many. The explosive devices are both partners' triggers. Then, to add gas to the flame, one explosion sets off a chain reaction until the whole field is charred and burning.

In real life, these land mines are simple things like running late, not taking out the garbage, a disappointed look, or a tense tone of voice. The chain reaction is the response to the initial explosion, which is often something like "What do you mean I gave you a look? I didn't give you a look. *You* were the one who gave me a look!"

We can't get rid of all the land mines, but we can work to disengage from our triggers and wounds. If one partner was often yelled at by a parent, for example, they will be more likely to shut down when their adult partner yells. The more we tend to these old wounds, the more we can stop the chain reactions. When we do not react, our partners have nothing to fight against, and the chain reaction slows and eventually stops.

Giving my clients perspectives about our psychological nature and what creates closeness in relationships has helped them slow down their reactions and bring more empathy to their partners. Knowing that many of our reactions are inherited from our parents and generations of relatives who faced stressful situations, we can find compassion for ourselves too. The author and spiritual practitioner Douglas Abrams had the opportunity to spend a week with the Dalai Lama and Desmond Tutu, two of the most powerful spiritual leaders of our time, to compile *The Book of Joy*. He wrote about the potential for harmony when we pause to empathize, rather than react. We can shift, he says, "from self righteous indignation—*how dare s/he speak to me like that*, to compassionate understanding—*he or she must be very tired to speak to me like that.*" (Abrams, 2016)

Learning to open my heart and be curious about someone else's experience in the heat of the moment has been an important part of my path. Jumping to negative conclusions and initiating self-protection mode is all too easy. In an attempt to feel safe and powerful, it is common to instinctively defend or threaten. But in doing this, we cut off the connection and end up unsafe and disempowered.

Compassionate curiosity is a foundation I use myself and bring to all my clients. It helps lessen reactivity, which supports deeper connection and ignites passion. Compassionate curiosity involves putting yourself in another's shoes by asking open questions to make sure we understand their experience. This is an integral perspective to hold as we approach the following fundamentals my clients have found most helpful in their relationships.

FUNDAMENTAL 1: BE ON THE SAME TEAM

Couples often get into a tit-for-tat or transactional way of relating. The conversation might go something like: "You were out one night last week, so I get a night out this week." Or "I took out the garbage, so it's your turn to do the laundry." This can extend into intimacy as well—keeping track of who has scratched whose back and when, who makes an effort to initiate sex, and who has "given" more orgasms. It can start to seem like the only way for one person to get more of what they want is for the other person to have less—someone needs to give up their time, money, or energy for someone else to have what they want.

This idea pits us against each other and creates a dynamic in which, instead of being on the same team, we are competing in a zero-sum game. When couples feel like they are on different teams, they are more likely to fight and try to protect, or even steal, their precious resources. They are less likely to collaborate and think creatively.

Abby Medcalf is a TEDx speaker, author, and psychologist. In her TEDx Talk, "The Real Reasons Relationships Fail," she says one of the main ways couples fall into the opposite-team dynamic is by keeping score. "When this happens," she says "someone has to lose." A point or score for one becomes bad for the other, rather than being good for both. When relationships become a win/lose battle, I have seen intimacy fade faster than dumping a dirt pile on a fire. As we shift from opposite- to same-team thinking, we start to explore how each partner can get more of what they want, increasing fulfillment for both. Rather than focusing on our own needs, we start to think in "win-wins,"—what would be mutually beneficial. (Medcalf, 2020)

This way of thinking about relationships is a perspective shift that wives Meghan and Erika Neeley have made in their own relationship and guide their clients through as LGBTQ relationship coaches. "We orient around full choosing and a full-body Yes for both people, rather than focusing on compromise," Meghan said as we discussed win-win dynamics together. Although we often hear relationships require compromise, the Neeleys find this can be taken to the extreme, leaving people feeling squashed or suffocated in relationships.

We cannot always get what we want, but we can ask ourselves questions that open our minds to possibilities, rather than focus on limitations. One question the Neeleys bring to their clients and their own relationship is "What would it look like for us both to have what we want?" As we ask questions like this, our minds open to new options. When we stay on the same team, we can collaborate and co-create solutions that are uplifting.

PRACTICE

Try on the perspective that wins for a partner or loved one can be a win for you too. This framing shifts the perspective to reveal more possibility, which allows for more creativity. Choose something you have been struggling with and initiate a conversation that starts with "How can we both win and have more of what we want?" Give each person a chance to feel heard, and then negotiate and collaborate when a solution is not immediately obvious. Do your best to explore this with care and creativity, rather than defensiveness and resentment.

FUNDAMENTAL 2: DIFFERENCES CAN BRING YOU CLOSER

People often choose partners as a yin to their yang, a light to their dark, peanut butter to their jelly. Down the road, these differences can become frustrating. But differences, while sometimes uncomfortable and challenging, bring variety and support we would miss if we chose a partner more like ourselves. Differences evoke inspiration and stretch us into trying new things and expanding our worldview.

That said, even simple differences can be painful. Doug Brackmann, PhD, and author of the book *Driven,* appeared on the *Man Alive* podcast Episode 202. During our discussion, he distinguished between two types of people: farmers and hunters. (Brackmann 2021)

We established that I have characteristics of a hunter. I am often in action and looking for the next thing to do, whereas a farmer type moves slowly and has an easy time relaxing. He asked if I had been in a relationship with a farmer type. I remembered packing for trips with my ex-husband, whose pace was *different* from mine. It took years for me to devise a plan to stop resenting his languid tempo. I came up with the idea to divide our tasks for a trip. The first time we experimented with this, I finished hours earlier than he did. I relaxed and read a book instead of stewing in frustration for hours, which not only pissed me off, but turned me off.

It's not that my ex's farmer pace is wrong, but it caused tension between us because we were on different ends of the spectrum. Alison Armstrong, a teacher who helps women understand men and is the author of many books, including *Making Sense of Men*, talks and writes about how women tend to compare themselves to men. In a workshop I attended, she said, "Too often, women feel that men come up short. Women see men as hairy, misbehaving women." While this statement strikes me as hilarious, there are also serious implications. When someone, of any gender, feels judged by another's differing standards, it creates painful disagreements and long-standing resentments.

Rather than seeing differences as liabilities, couples can start to focus on how each person's differences benefit the couple. My ex's attention to detail saved us from being disqualified on rental and financial applications. My quick pace and thinking ahead allowed us to visit many fantastic schools for our kid when we moved to a new state.

A conversation to celebrate differences can start with each person making a list of the differences that create struggles. The next step is to sit down and ask for each difference, "How can we shift the struggle so it feels better for both of us?" No difference is too small to address. If you feel upset by it, consider a solution that works better. Small things may be:

- I like to turn off the lights, and you leave them on.

- You spend more of our shared money on clothes than I want you to.

- When we share food, you take the last bite without asking me.

Bigger issues may be things like:

- I am trying to use positive language with our kids, and you reprimand them.

- I value spending time with my family, and you do not want to.

- I want our sex to feel more intimate, and you don't seem to care.

Issues may not get "solved" immediately, but the willingness to consider new solutions goes a long way toward each person feeling more understood and more willing to be collaborative.

PRACTICE

Have a conversation about a difference that has caused frustration. Rather than focusing on the irritation or upset the desire causes, acknowledge the benefits each person brings to the relationship as a result of the difference. The more you can celebrate each other, the more win-wins you can create. You can use the question from Fundamental 1 to collaborate or negotiate if you decide to try something new. After a conversation like this, it is helpful to write down notes and/or agreements about what you discover. This way you can look back at them together, rather than having a battle between each person's memory.

FUNDAMENTAL 3: ASSUME THE BEST ABOUT EACH OTHER RATHER THAN THE WORST

From 2003 to 2011, I co-created and taught the Authentic Woman Experience, a series of workshops for women in romantic relationships with men. We distinguished two ways women could respond when they were upset with a man. The first was to assume the worst and criticize or cut him down. The second was to see the best in him and remind him of that version of himself. I imagine which one gets the better response is obvious!

"Assuming the worst" is imagining negative intentions for someone's actions. Clients I have worked with have said or heard things like, "You meant to hurt me," or "You did that on purpose because you knew it would drive me crazy." Statements like these assume a negative intent behind the action. Looking deeper, we can see these assumptions are based in hurt and fear, which lead to distrust and defensiveness.

The shift we can make is from "assuming the worst" and building a case against someone to "assuming the best" and getting curious. Instead of assuming negative intentions, we can actually imagine our partner had positive intentions, but fell short for some reason. We get curious about that reason by asking questions with care and connection, rather than with blame and accusation. This simple shift has a profound impact.

Instead of saying something like "When you were late last night, I know you were getting back at me for staying out later than I said I would last week," we can shift to "When you came home late last night, I was worried you were upset with me for being late last week so I wanted to check in. Are you upset with me?"

Rather than believing our negative thoughts, we can acknowledge that at least some of our hurt feelings come from what we tell ourselves about a situation, rather than the situation itself. We add our assessments and judgments on top of the objective situation. I may tell myself that my partner leaves his laundry in a pile in the laundry room because he expects me to do it. But he may or may not expect me to do it. I add my assessment to his action of leaving his clothes in a pile.

Instead of adding assessments, we can explore our reactions beyond our surface thoughts. We can meditate, exercise, talk with a friend, and do therapy or coaching to discover why we feel upset. Then we can bring vulnerability to the conversation, rather than accusation. We can ask curious questions instead of bringing righteousness about someone's intentions.

PRACTICE
To practice assuming the best, consider a situation with a person you care about, with whom you've been upset. What ideas do you have about why they did what they did? If these ideas do not assume the best—*that the person cares about you and has positive intentions toward you*—try on the "assume the best" framing. Then get curious about what happened for this person. Recently, a client told me he was stood up on a date. He later found out his date ended up in the hospital and did not have a way to let him know. It may not always be this extreme, but relationships will always stay more connected when we assume the best and get curious, instead of assuming the worst.

FUNDAMENTAL 4: SHARE *WHY* TO DEEPEN UNDERSTANDING
I have had many heated conversations when, just as the fight was about to blow up, my partner or I paused and shared *why*

we were fighting for our side. This has quelled the flames and caused a shift from fierce anger to teary compassion.

In the example with my ex-husband in the introduction of this book, we were fighting about water bottles. He wanted to buy one, but I did not want him to. The content we were fighting about, the water bottle, was surrounded by an invisible layer of *why* we were fighting about it. He was focused on survival because we were about to attend a festival in the desert where there is no water to drink unless you bring it. Dehydration can be deadly. I was focused on saving money and trying to do my part to decrease the Texas-sized island of plastic in the ocean. In this case, his attention on personal survival was pitted against my attention on planetary survival. An additional dose of financial fear was on my end as well. Unfortunately, at that time, we did not have a mature conversation in which our *why*s brought us closer.

When a client wanted to feel more inspired, he wanted to take a trip with his guy friends. His wife felt hurt. I guided him to share *why* he wanted this, in addition to simply sharing that he did. As he told her he had been feeling dull and wanted to make sure he was not on course for a mid-life crisis—and blowing up his life—she softened. He emphasized he was doing this for himself, but also to care for her and their relationship. He reported back that by adding this explanation, she was much more understanding and supportive.

In the kink and BDSM communities, the *why* is a part of the experience that is not skipped. In the example I previously shared about people who want to be tied up, there are a multitude of reasons why they want this—from wanting pain to surrender or even to feel cared about. Cleo DuBois, a BDSM-kink educator encouraged her students to "go beyond the checklist, to find the heart of your [partner's] desires." Finding the heart of a desire allows for staying connected and having transformative experiences. (Dubois, 2022)

It is easy to doubt the health or well-being of people who explore kink and BDSM and imagine they are just playing out old wounds. In his book, *Recovering the Rapture: Rethinking God, Sex, and Death in a World That's Lost Its Mind*, flow-state researcher Jamie Wheal, whom I mentioned earlier in the book, found otherwise. He writes that those who participate in kink and BDSM tend to rate healthy on the most widely used psychological model for assessing wellness through personality traits. We can build on the wisdom of the BDSM community, knowing that even if we do not want to go to these extremes, they practice a solid communication strategy that benefits any couple. (Wheal, 2021)

PRACTICE
The next time you have a desire your partner does not like or understand, tell them *why* you want it. Similarly, next time your partner has a desire that does not make sense to you, take the time to ask about your partner's *why*.

FUNDAMENTAL 5: USE DESIRES, *NOT* COMPLAINTS, TO CREATE MORE CONNECTION
I remember a therapy session with a partner when our therapist pointed out that I spent more time complaining about what I did not want than saying what I did want. It was

humbling, and I resisted his assessment at first. But over time, I saw that while I would initially bring my heartfelt desires, I would then resort to complaining. For example, I wanted to feel more connected in our sex life, but after feeling unheard, I talked more about my frustration than my excitement and inspiration. I told myself I had tried to bring my inspiration and that since it had not worked, all I could do was complain. But this is never true. We actually don't ever have to complain. We can always share our desires instead.

For my ex, my complaint evoked shame and a sense that he could not make me happy. As I focused on what was *not* working, rather than appreciating what was, he felt rejected. I have since realized, through personal growth work and supporting clients, that letting go of complaints and criticism can feel like giving up on or betraying ourselves. I remember fearing that if someone did not know I was suffering, they would not want to change. But inspiration has more power to shift a situation than negativity.

For many of us, complaining is a bad habit, left over from our youth. In the United States, people often bond through complaining. A world of desires opens up, however, when we put more attention on what we want than what we don't. When people feel less blamed, they are more likely to want to collaborate. This has created an upward spiral for many couples I have worked with.

PRACTICE

The next time you have a complaint, take some time to look deeper. What is the desire beneath what you are complaining about? If you are tired of someone leaving clothes on the floor, you could share about how a clean room would allow you to relax and (maybe) even feel more turned on! It can be hard to tap into desires when there is a storehouse of past resentments, but if you keep looking, you will find them.

FUNDAMENTAL 6: UN-DEFEND YOURSELF

One of my favorite and most often recommended books is called *Undefended Love*, by Jett Psaris and Marlena Lyons. I read it in my twenties when I was working on my psychology degree. In my thirties, I left our five-month-old baby with my husband and, breast pump in tow, went to the Undefended Love workshop. I wanted to see if it could support us to feel more understood by each other. Our differences seemed to feel bigger after becoming parents. (Psaris and Lyons 2000)

A premise of the book is that trying to prove or defend ourselves creates distance and is an illusory battle. This is important because many fights start with one person accusing the other of something. The receiver of the accusation then starts defending. We fight about our perceptions of each other, rather than hearing each other's pain and struggle. Granted, it is challenging to hear pain through blame, and we can learn to shift accusations to vulnerable statements. But we can also un-defend—or disarm—ourselves and shift how we receive our partner's accusations. Seeing that a complaint reveals a struggle on the accuser's end, we can choose to explore the struggle, rather than get defensive. I will not claim this is easy, and it takes practice to master this, but it has saved many relationships.

One of my clients had a partner who accused her of being selfish. "You don't think about anyone else. You just do what you want to do," her partner said. We explored her initial response, which was to defend herself and point out how she was not selfish. Then we practiced imagining what her partner was feeling. When we stepped into his shoes, we saw that he was afraid of being abandoned. When she made important decisions without consulting him, he felt afraid of being left behind. Rather than vulnerably admitting this, he would blow up and call her selfish. When she stopped defending herself, and instead brought care and concern, letting him know she could understand why he was afraid she'd leave, his accusations ceased.

Thinking that if we do not defend ourselves, we will be forever defined by an accusation is common. What we do not realize is that defending exacerbates the accusation, whereas exploring it with humility brings the understanding that dissipates it.

PRACTICE
The next time you are tempted to defend yourself, consider what your partner is struggling with but not saying. Get curious and ask caring questions to understand their challenge. See if you can let go of taking the accusation personally and consider that your partner is feeling vulnerable. We will always learn more about our partners and ourselves when we do not choose to engage in a battle of defensiveness.

CHANGE YOUR THOUGHTS, CHANGE YOUR SEX LIFE
The ways we think and speak about ourselves and our partners have a powerful impact on intimacy and sex. The great part about this is that we can cultivate the capacity to witness our

thoughts and choose the ones we want to put attention on. As we strengthen the perspectives that empower our compassion for others, our actions become more respectful and create more harmony. This bodes well for our relationships.

A famous quote often attributed to Lao Tzu is:

> *Watch your thoughts, they become your words. Watch your words, they become your actions. Watch your actions, they become your habits. Watch your habits, they become your character. Watch your character, it becomes your destiny.*

The more we are able to witness our thoughts and consciously choose the words that come out of our mouths, the stronger and more intimate our relationships become. To support this in your life, pick a fundamental from this chapter that you see you could improve on and explore the practice. If you have a partner, talk about it and explore it together. Check in regularly to assess your challenges and successes, whether making notes on your own or in a conversation together. Ask others whether they notice the changes you are attempting to make and listen with humility to what they see in you. This kind of honesty and willingness to grow goes a long way to creating relationships that are caring, kind, and passionate.

CHAPTER 11

CONSCIOUS RELATING TOOLS

As we become more conscious in our relationships, sex serves a purpose beyond procreation and pleasure. Relationships become a vehicle for our growth, inspiring us to consider who and how we want to be. I call this conscious relating.

Seeing that many adults in this current era grew up in the age of Disney fantasies and rom-coms, I realized that our relationship examples were not conscious. The media showed "happily ever after," and most of our parents did not study communication or emotional intelligence. We gleaned that love *should* stay steady and sex *should* stay passionate over time. This has caused relationship conversations to feel shameful for many of my clients. Why would we have these conversations if everything is supposed to magically feel good? Isn't having them a sign that we are doing something wrong?

For relationships to stay intimate and passionate, couples need to prioritize conscious conversations as a part of our relationship hygiene, similar to physical hygiene habits like brushing our teeth or sweeping our floors. Questions like "What could I do so you feel more loved today?" or "What would have made last night's sex even better for you?" could be integrated into our daily routines. In conscious relating, we continually get to know more about each other, even after decades, rather than concluding that we already know someone. We can have conversations to digest emotions like disappointment, fear, and anger that otherwise weigh us down and disconnect us.

In the introduction, I wrote that some people believe our culture has outgrown marriage. I believe, however, that we have not matured *enough* to make marriage or long-term relationships work. The following tools are pathways to the mature honesty it takes to grow closer, rather than apart. These conscious relating methods come from my decades of training in communication, emotional intelligence, authentic relating, meditation, masculine/feminine dynamics, and more. They are often simple, though not necessarily easy. At times, they will feel like work. At times, you'll be surprised by the connection and sexiness they evoke. Remember, there is no way to get this right. Instead, practice revealing and receiving vulnerable honesty and you will open to the depth of intimacy many couples never find.

SIX HEALTHY, VITAL, AND PASSIONATE RELATIONSHIP TOOLS

1. AGREEMENTS

When I ask most couples why they are together, they tend to look at each other with an uncertain shrug. They say, "We got together because we love each other," or "We got together because we wanted to have a family," or "We got together because that's what people do." After marriage vows are made, many of us leave things to chance. We do not revisit our agreements or consider them in our day-to-day life, so vows remain theoretical, if not altogether lost.

However, the more intentional we are, the more likely our relationships are to thrive for the long haul. I was working with a client who was trying to have conversations with his wife about the sex he wanted. As I supported him to get more vulnerable, she made comments about his desires that felt hurtful. She did not intend to make him feel bad, but she responded with her fears, rather than asking curious questions to discover more about his desires.

Knowing that a sense of safety is needed for connection to deepen, I felt this couple would benefit from making agreements about how they spoke to each other. I guided him to let his wife know he wanted to talk about *how* they respond to each other, especially during moments of fear and upset. They made an agreement to shift from interrupting each other and unconsciously spouting their fears to doing their best to listen to each other fully and be more curious. They courageously created the safety that allowed them to take more risks in their conversations.

We often have to go back to the basics of how we speak, listen, and respond to each other. We can use agreements to commit to do our best to be present, respectful, and vulnerable, rather than dismissive or critical. Agreements can be made with roles as well. Taking on roles that stem from a patriarchal culture or familial norms, rather than exploring each couple's unique dynamic, often creates resentment and disconnection.

Agreements about chores and tasks can shift a couple from the pain of expectations and assumptions to the joy of connection and collaboration. Agreements are also powerful for exploring and creating the balance of autonomy and communion we need to feel close. Couples commonly have different needs for alone and together time, so creating agreements around how and when these happen can ease anxiety.

Making explicit agreements does not mean we will keep them 100 percent of the time. We all make mistakes. Most couples will have to iterate on agreements until they hone in on what works. When an agreement is broken, we bring as much vulnerable honesty as we can muster. I suggest couples write down agreements because they can refer back to something more concrete than memories. This cuts down on disagreements.

When desires remain implicit and no agreements are made, frustration and disappointment build and intimacy fades. Creating agreements gives each person a way to have their desires more likely to be met. If you need support to accept the inevitability of a partner making mistakes, review the Assume the Best section in the previous chapter. If you need to clear up a broken agreement, check out the DEAR process below.

PRACTICE

To start making agreements with a partner, make a list of situations that cause the most tension or upset. Once you have each made your lists, schedule a time to share them. Practice speaking from a humble place, recognizing that "it takes two to tango." Rather than being righteous or blaming, remain vulnerable and honor the fact that we always play a role in any dynamic. Note: There are situations when people will be unwilling to or incapable of being fully honest or vulnerable. If you find this to be the case, please get support. It is common to fall in love and realize that a partner is on the autistic spectrum or has narcissistic tendencies. Couples might need professional help with these dynamics.

Here is an example agreement:

We agree to listen to each other through the eyes and ears of love and care, rather than fear. When we find ourselves stuck in fear, we acknowledge it, rather than let it run the show. We slow down or take a break in order to get back to the love we have for each other.

As I said before, we will never be perfect at keeping agreements like this. The point of agreements is to keep us oriented toward our desires and commitments and remind us to get back on course when we stray.

2. USER GUIDE

Many adults I know joke about how great it would be to have a guide to their partner's moods, frustrations, and upsets. Very few realize they could actually have one. A User Guide is the key! It is like the manual included with a new appliance, but it shows us how our partners are wired and what idiosyncrasies they have. This is the guide we wish we were handed when we met our partners and the one they wish they were handed when they met us. Creating this guide to our and our partner's habits and patterns allows us to collaborate on best practices so we can bypass recurring upsets and conflicts.

When a partner tells me that an appliance in my house does not work well, our User Guide reminds us that I am likely to feel criticized and ashamed. Knowing this allows us both to adjust. He can be more conscious about how and when he brings his assessments. I can remind myself that my choice of inanimate objects says nothing about my worthiness. As we map out what happens during upsets and frustrations, we get to the front side of arguments, rather than being blindsided by them and ending up in a downward spiral that pulls us apart.

Another benefit of creating a User Guide is that we can identify what helps us feel cared for and supported in challenging moments. As crazy as this may sound, it helps when my partner tells me that even though he does not like my choice of a vacuum cleaner, he still loves me. We all have past wounds that cause reactions that can seem overblown. The more familiar we are with how these wounds cause us to feel criticized or unsupported, the more we can work together to make requests, rather than defend or attack.

In couples, there are often times when someone simply wants to be heard or understood but their partner tries to fix or solve the challenges. With this captured as a pattern in the User Guide, we can come up with alternatives that maintain feelings of respect and connection. After listening to my TEDx Talk, *What 1,000 Men's Tears Reveal about the Crisis Between Men and Women*, a friend thanked me for highlighting this cycle in her marriage. *"My husband has been asking me to listen, rather than make suggestions for how things could go better,"* she said, *"but I didn't get it until now."* They could note this cycle in their User Guide. When he was not being listened to in the way he desired, he could reference their guide and make a request. Referring back to a written document can relieve some of the vulnerability we might feel when reminding our partners about our optimal conditions for feeling cared for.

PRACTICE

You can create your User Guide by writing down situations in which you have felt mad, disappointed, or wanted a different response. Write down the response you would have liked instead. When you are complete with this list, write down any repeating disagreements the list does not cover. If you are single, you can explore your dynamics with friends, family, and colleagues. If you are doing this with a partner, share your lists with each other and brainstorm ideas to shift these dynamics. When you share, remember, it is more effective to bring a request about the response you desire, rather than a complaint. The User Guide goes a long way toward ending recurring struggles. You can proactively build on your new awareness by creating agreements. See Foundation 1 for guidance.

3. CPR

The CPR works with the proven power of visualization. Multiple studies have demonstrated that visualizing an event or outcome causes neural networks to form similarly to how they would if the event or outcome actually occurred. We can tap into the power of visualization to create experiences by envisioning and writing down what we want to happen. Doing this with a partner helps us focus our joint attention on the outcomes we desire, rather than complaining or hoping these outcomes happen. [3]

A CPR—a written document structured to set intentions—is a powerful tool for this practice. There are three parts—context, purpose, and results. I write CPRs before taking trips, leading workshops, at the beginning of a year, and I wrote one for the birth of my child. The process of creating a CPR can be extremely clarifying for a couple.

When using a CPR to envision how we want an experience to go, we write the results section first. We make a list of what we want to happen in the past tense, as though it already happened. Some example results I have written were:

- The birth was smooth, and we were all safe and healthy the whole way through.

- During our vacation, we felt more connected than ever.

- Every participant had an insight that will translate into deeper connection with a partner, friend, or family member.

---

3   For further information, check out Tracy C. Ekeocha's "The Effects of Visualization & Guided Imagery in Sports Performance."

In the purpose statement, Ian Rhett, founder of Success Thinc, writes it "is structured to distill and synthesize the results you declared into a statement that describes the reason(s) you are doing the activity—and what way(s) of being will have those results appear." (Rhett, 2016)

In other words, we distill results into a statement that shows why and how we will accomplish them. The "how" in this case focuses more on how we are being rather than what we are doing. Rhett gives an example structure:

- The purpose of . . . *(insert activity)*

- is to . . . *(insert outcome)*

- through . . . *(insert way(s) of being)*

- such that . . . *(insert big picture outcome)*

Here is an example purpose statement: "*The purpose of taking this trip together is to deepen our connection through caring for and being curious about each other, such that we ignite the intimacy that keeps us together for another thirty plus years.*"

The context section of the CPR is a simple word or phrase that points toward the results and purpose. It encapsulates the sentiment of the outcomes we desire. On a trip I took to Hawaii after my child was born and I felt like an exhausted mother, my context was "the phoenix." In that phase of life, I wanted to remember that I could feel renewed and vital, rather than defeated and depleted. As I decided what to do each day, this context supported me. It led me to swim with dolphins, visit black sand beaches, and walk on lava fields. Instead of *hoping* for great experiences, my context guided me to make decisions based on what was important to me. My days were intentional and powerful as a result.

PRACTICE

Pick a situation that is important to you and start to visualize what you want to happen. Use the guidance from the above examples to write a CPR. If you have a partner, you could create one for a joint experience. If you are doing this alone, I suggest sharing your CPR with someone you feel close to. They can witness, support, and celebrate your goals. After writing the CPR, keep it close by during the situation so you can refer back to it and stay focused on your desired outcomes. [4]

4. DEAR PROCESS

One of the ongoing struggles couples must face in relationships is that apologies do not always take away the hurt of a painful action. Most of us have been on the receiving end of an apology where someone has closed body language or a rude tone. We see crossed arms and a defiant attitude and wonder whether the apology is sincere. Some apologies are truly insincere—begrudgingly spoken to save face without compassion or responsibility. Other apologies are heartfelt or sincere, but even so, they are not effective. The thing about apologies is that even the best ones don't often

---

4 For practice on this, check out "From Mental Power to Muscle Power—Gaining Strength by Using the Mind" by V. K. Ranganathan, V. Siemionow, J. Z. Liu, V. Sahgal, and G. H. Yue.

succeed in repairing a relationship or cultivating more trust and connection.

The words "I'm sorry" have rung empty to me so many times that I started looking for a better way to apologize. I prefer a tool called the DEAR process. This is one of my favorite ways to restore trust and connection, and I frequently use it with couples. I learned it in my twenties from Mark Michael Lewis, a life coach who focuses on life optimization. The process is initiated by someone who has broken an agreement—*building on Fundamental 1: Agreements.* It gives the receiver in the process a chance to share upsets and desires, and they can choose a repair that dissolves any residue. The process also includes a recommitment to or renegotiation of agreements if necessary. (Lewis, 2003)

I'll describe the method, but first, I want to demonstrate its power. I remember a meeting when someone arrived late. The norm, when someone walks in late is, "Sorry I'm late" and people move on. But this can leave lasting breaks in trust and cause disrespect or frustration detrimental to future relating and collaborating. Although the lateness did not create a major breach of trust, it did have an impact. Many of us were anxious to get started because we had a limited amount of time.

Even though it seemed counterintuitive to spend more time on this, we used the DEAR process, knowing it could prevent future breakdowns and cohere the team. Those who felt negatively impacted spoke up and were heard. In this case, the fact that the latecomer acknowledged and showed care about the impact was enough of an amends. Other times, the recommitment or renegotiation phase clears the air. The receiver can also make a request for something meaningful to rebuild trust or even something that would be fun to receive. I have requested small things, like flowers and coffee, and larger things, like requesting a partner have a conversation with a friend or therapist to get to the bottom of why a behavior happened.

Here is how you can use the process:

D: When you have broken an agreement, *declare* that you have done so. Rather than saying "I'm sorry," include the specifics of what the agreement was and how you broke it. This is a simple statement to acknowledge what happened, rather than an apology.

E: *Explore* the impact of breaking the agreement on the other person. This is a chance to ask about how trust or connection was broken. Do your best to hear and understand the other's upset. Try to listen without taking it personally.

A: Make *amends.* Ask the person impacted what would allow them to feel better—or *possibly even grateful*—that the agreement was broken. They may not immediately have an answer, so be patient. You can brainstorm together.

R: *Recommit or renegotiate* the original agreement: Check to see whether the original agreement still feels viable to each person. If it is, make a recommitment. If it is not, renegotiate to create an agreement both people feel good about. Note: If an agreement has been broken multiple times and trust is broken, there may need to be a deeper exploration of the underlying causes.

PRACTICE

Think about a recent time when you had a less than desirable impact on someone you care about. Ask them if they would be willing to try the DEAR process. You don't have to pretend to be an expert. Be honest that this is new to you and let them know you would like to try a new way to reconnect and repair beyond an apology. After you complete the process, ask them for feedback about how it felt in relation to an apology.

One pitfall to watch out for is trying to get someone else to acknowledge that they have broken an agreement. This process works best when it is self-initiated. With that said, two people could create an agreement that allows either person to initiate or ask to use the DEAR process to clean up a broken agreement.

5. RACE TO VULNERABILITY

Vulnerability often involves admitting what makes us feel unlovable or unworthy, so it is not most people's idea of fun. My clients find it challenging and even with twenty-five years of practice, my face can still get hot and my mouth dry when I reveal vulnerable honesty. However, I know it is one of the fastest paths to heal hurt and conflict.

My friend and colleague, Shelly Birger, created a game called the Race to Vulnerability with her husband to make vulnerability more palatable. In their family, the one who is vulnerable first "wins." Think of a moment when partners are disappointed in each other, and they are not feeling supported. Tones get harsh and words become critical. With the Race to Vulnerability game, instead of escalating or retreating, one person can simply stop the argument and get vulnerable. "Hey," one could say, "I don't like how I said that. I apologize for speaking to you that way." Whoever gets vulnerable first is the winner!

When I asked Shelly if they have a prize for this she said, "No prize. Just a better relationship and bragging rights." But couples can also create a prize. For example, the one who gets honest first doesn't have to cook dinner for a few nights or gets to choose what to do for the next date night! With or without a prize, the faster we bring vulnerability, the less trust we break and the less cleanup there is to do.

During a rare and heated fight with a partner, we realized we were not getting anywhere. We both agreed it would be helpful to share what felt most vulnerable about the topic for us. We knew this would likely resolve our disagreement, but we each still felt resistant and irritated. We took an hour break to find a more centered and caring state and came back together to get honest and drop our defenses.

As we sat on the couch, at first not even wanting to look at each other, we started sharing about our hurts and fears. Rather than fighting for our positions or blaming each other, we were tender. We each filled in the simple sentence stem: "What feels vulnerable about this for me is . . ." Both of our hearts softened as we understood the deeper layers at play. Not only did it stop the argument, but we felt even closer and more loving toward each other than before it happened. It was clearing out cobwebs we hadn't even realized were there.

Bringing vulnerability, rather than defensiveness, is one of the fastest ways to end conflict. At times, I suggest my clients simply say "Ouch," when their feelings are hurt, rather than responding with content about their hurt. This makes it so there is nothing to fight against and avoids getting caught in a gridlock of arguing about content.

PRACTICE
The next time you are in a conflict, practice being the first one to get a bit more vulnerable. Take a deep breath and complete the sentence "I know this is hard for both of us. What is vulnerable about this for me is . . ." You can also request that each of you complete the sentence. I have found that when I am willing to be vulnerable first, others are likely to follow.

6. DAILY APPRECIATION
I have seen the difference between relationships where communication is full of complaint and nagging versus communication based in gratitude and appreciation. In the former, the mood starts to feel like an explosive battleground or a deadened graveyard. Bitterness and resentment festers and partners end up resentful and defeated. Sound familiar? This obviously kills passion, and it sadly eats away at the underlying respect needed to foster care and connection. It sets a downward spiral in motion that is difficult to recover from.

A daily, healthy regimen of appreciation creates an upward spiral in a relationship. One of the simplest ways to keep connection thriving is to put attention on what we are grateful for and enjoy about a partner. There are times when we have to dig to find this—beneath the daily annoyances that fill our awareness—but we can cultivate the skill of shifting our attention. Appreciation is exponential, so the more we appreciate, the more we become inspired to take care of each other.

We can start to recognize and acknowledge the deeper contribution a partner's support brings, rather than expecting to have our needs met and tasks handled. This means that when someone takes out the garbage or washes the dishes, rather than focusing our attention on who has done more—and coming up the winner—the focus shifts to gratitude. It might seem miniscule, but from a perspective of thankfulness, gaining ten minutes to take a load off, or the opportunity to smell delicious food instead of taking out stinky garbage, is an actual cause for celebration.

We can always appreciate something about a partner. In a sexual context, I remind my clients that even if we don't like the way someone is touching us, we could feel grateful that they are touching us at all. When you start here, appreciating a partner's willingness or care and making mature requests for what feels good, everyone can get more of what they want.

PRACTICE

I recommend appreciating your partner on random occasions, but a scheduled daily appreciation routine goes a long way. A great time to do this is at night before bed, but it could be done any time during the day. Face-to-face is the best way to do this, but it could also happen over the phone or through a text message.

Give each person a chance to appreciate three things about the other from the day—or the day before if you do it in the morning. Remember to dig deep if you have to. Appreciating that your partner puts up with your idiosyncrasies or has taken on something you now don't have to do is a great appreciation. Remember that the more you appreciate, the more likely you'll be to get more support.

Note: If you really cannot find anything to appreciate about a partner, it is time to get some relationship help and recover some of the effusiveness that likely saturated your brain in the honeymoon phase.

TRY A CONSCIOUS RELATING TOOL

These tools help us to be more intentional about our goals and desires. They also help us clean up hurts that would fester and turn into resentments. Try these exercises with a partner to practice opening up lines of communication, trust, and aliveness. You could set up a time to try one tool each week or each month, whatever feels right to you. If you do not have a partner, try them with a close friend or family member. Remember to be gentle with yourself as you are new to practicing them. They are likely to feel awkward at first, but they are powerful for keeping connection and passion alive!

FINAL THOUGHTS

———

Relationships are complicated. Not only do we face personal challenges, but political and cultural ones as well. We have homes, careers, health, kids, and finances to handle and daily struggles to navigate. The act of relating, on the other hand, can actually be quite simple.

It takes practice, but we can be more conscious and stop acting out from our young parts. We do not have to defend or negate. We do not have to judge or attack. We do not have to prioritize fear and our adaptive child's stories over love and the adult's learned wisdom. We will no doubt be tempted to do all of these, but we *can* stop ourselves and make conscious choices.

We can choose to open our hearts and see from another's perspective. We can be willing to reveal and hear vulnerable truths. We can set aside righteousness and blame. We can wait to speak until we believe our words will do as little harm as possible. Of course, simple is not always easy, but we can create relationships from these foundations. And when we do, romantic relationships become one of most potent opportunities to evolve our young and fearful parts. The pain and suffering that is activated in our relationships can heal past wounds we did not have the strength to face when we were young. We get to experience more love and peace in ourselves and our relationships.

RELATIONAL ALCHEMY

John Welwood is a psychotherapist and author of one of my favorite books, *Love and Awakening: The Sacred Path of Intimate Relationship*. "When we view the journey of romantic relationships with the context of growth," he writes, "our relationships become deeper and more meaningful." He describes this as "relational alchemy." This has been profound for me. When I contextualize a conflict I go through in terms of growth, I become more relaxed and optimistic. As I consider how my relationship and I can evolve through this conflict, I discover opportunities and gifts I was not originally aware of. This has allowed me to panic less and feel more empowered. Bringing in the context of growth can shift us from the "why me?" paradigm to the "how can this situation support me to become more whole and healthy?" paradigm. (Welwood, 1997)

The historical version of alchemy involved the attempt to transform lead, a base metal, into gold, a precious metal. In a relationship context, we are transforming fear into love. The more honest we get about the layers of our inner experience, the easier it becomes to speak and act from love, rather than fear. From love, we are more patient, understanding, and heartfelt. Instead of taking a partner for granted, blaming them, or speaking from the inner critic's voice, we can cultivate the capacity to respond in caring, respectful ways, staying connected even amidst challenges. This is relationship gold.

Twenty years ago, I met the man who would become my husband and then ex-husband. At that point, I was much more emotionally unbalanced. My mind often spun out in fear. I felt strong desires and dislikes. I swung from feeling loving and wanting connection to feeling detached and wanting freedom. At times, I was warm. At times, I was cold. Sometimes, I was rigid about my needs. Other times, I lost myself by giving in to what he wanted.

I have definitely matured, but these complicated inner realities have not disappeared. I still hear and feel the pull of my immature parts. Most importantly, I relate to these parts differently now. The commitment I made after my divorce—*to not speak until I knew I would move a conversation toward more love and understanding*—inspired me to step into a capacity I was unaware I had. I can now maintain a centered and conscious demeanor that is respectful and loving, even when I am upset. I use many tools and practices daily, including those mentioned in this book. The simplest and most powerful tool I use when I am afraid or upset is the moment of pause and reminding myself of my commitment.

MATURITY AND OUR INNER DEMONS

Richard Schwartz, founder of Internal Family Systems, describes the maturity that now drives my way of acting as "Self-led." This means the parts of me that are hurt, angry, and fearful still shout at me. But the Self, the more essential aspect that has access to Schwartz's eight Cs—*compassion, curiosity, calm, clarity, courage, connectedness, confidence, and creativity*—runs the show. Even with decades of experience, every conflict or misunderstanding still feels like practice. I do not know if navigating upsets will ever come naturally, but that is less important than a commitment to act consciously. (IFS, 2022)

Schwartz writes "to experience this Self, there is no shortcut around our inner barbarians—those unwelcome parts of ourselves, such as hatred, rage, suicidal despair, fear, addictive need, racism and other prejudice, greed, as well as the somewhat less heinous feelings of ennui, guilt, depression, anxiety, self-righteousness, and self-loathing." Part of me cringes to read the long list of shadow aspects we have to navigate and the expert perspective that we cannot avoid them. I take comfort, however, in how impersonal this journey is. Remembering that we all have these "inner barbarians" helps us have more compassion for ourselves and others.

Schwartz, Marshank, Real, Merzel, and other wise teachers share the belief that we have to listen to and embrace *all* of our parts. As we discover the needs that drive these parts, they stop trying to run the show or wreak havoc on our lives. This has been the most challenging part for me and many of my clients: to love the parts of ourselves we have a hard time welcoming. Instead of blatantly resisting them or subtly denying them, we can practice listening to the unwelcome parts with acceptance and love. Receiving them this way eases their fight. We become freer to access the mature parts when we are not engaged in a battle with our young ones.

Couples will inevitably oscillate between joy and frustration because upsets are impossible to avoid. As we grow and become more conscious though, we gain more control over whether we unconsciously slip into habitual reactions or dynamics. When we learn to witness the young parts, rather than act them out, we can consciously choose a step that leads to connection. Although this kind of honesty does not mean a relationship will last forever, it means no one has to leave in a huff or with ill wishes. Our relationships can evolve in ways that are caring and respectful.

I BELIEVE YOU CAN CREATE A CONSCIOUS RELATIONSHIP

I believe we are more capable of being mature in our relationships than we realize. Even when it is not easy, we can commit to honestly love with maturity. Mature honesty is the foundation that allows all of our experiences, even hurt, fear, and anger, to become a doorway to deeper, more loving connection. Practicing vulnerable self-revealing creates a kind of intimacy where we get to feel understood, loved, and supported. I have been blown away by this, in ways I never imagined possible. It also creates passion that becomes hotter, more connected, and transcendent as time goes on. I know this is possible for all of us.

Please do not think there is something wrong with you if you get stuck, or if you find that you cannot do this on your own. I have been fortunate to work with dozens of guides, and I have spent thousands of hours exploring the habits and patterns that block me from loving and being loved. I still consult my guides on a regular basis, and I believe we all need help. No two relationships are the same, so there is not a one-size-fits-all answer to all relationship struggles. Take from this book what inspires you and leave what does not.

I offer many avenues of support, including my podcast, courses, and coaching. Feel free to reach out with questions, and I would love to hear your takeaways from reading the book.

I believe you can have loving, supportive, passionate relationships. The older I get, the more I see that this does not mean they always look how we thought they would. Conventional norms present a small box, with a limited number of options for love and relationships. I believe we get to choose our relationships based on what inspires and excites us. The more conscious we become, the more empowered we are to create these relationships.

For more Honest Sex resources, scan this QR code with your phone camera:

With love,
Shana

ACKNOWLEDGMENTS

———

This book would not have been possible without my incredible support network of colleagues, family, friends, and relational practice partners.

Thank you to everyone who has believed in me and engaged in mature honesty with me—especially in the vulnerable and challenging moments. Writing the book and walking this path has been a humbling and thrilling journey. I could not have learned to deepen connection and become more vulnerably honest on my own.

I stand on the shoulders of many leaders of the personal growth movement, psychologists, and spiritual teachers. I also have a cadre of guides and colleagues who support my growth and spiritual evolution.

Special thanks to:

My amazing editors—Jessica Carew Kraft for your worldly wisdom and your way with words, Katie Sigler for organizing my thoughts into coherent themes, Morgana Watson for being a tireless cheerleader, and Chuck Oexmann for helping me get it done!

Thank you, Eric Koester, for creating the Book Creators program and your endless enthusiasm in guiding us through the herculean process of finishing a book.

Thank you to my interviewees—Alicia Davon, Alyssa Morin, Jamie Wheal, John Gottman, Jordan Gray, Marcia Baczynski, Meghan Neeley, Michael Russer, Sarah Marshank, Susan Bratton, Susan Campbell, and Terrence Real—for not only spending time with me, but for spending decades cultivating your expertise and supporting the vulnerable growth and evolution of so many people.

Thank you to all my beta readers for your insightful suggestions. Special thanks to Alisha Musicant and Wouter Slegers. Your thorough reading and understanding of the content inspired me to clarify and deepen important concepts.

Mom and Dad—thank you for being the ground under me and reminding me that I can do anything I set my mind to.

Evelyn Birnbaum, Pamela Jay, Sarah Marshank—thank you for being my wise women spiritual guidance team who supports my mind, heart, body, and soul.

Tim James—thank you for being an amazing co-parent and practice partner, and the one with whom I made the most mistakes. I'm grateful we've grown so much and practice relating consciously.

Ari James—thank you for our daily practice of becoming more conscious and loving in our communication and our actions. I love you the mostest.

Alexis Sheppherd, Dan and Jenifer Ancona, Debra Artura, Jeanine Becker, Laura Wald, Megan Walrod, Nikki Pava, Rebecca Trobe, Steve McGraw—thank you for being thought partners and co-creators, and for years of authentic and vulnerable conversations that generate consistent growth.

Thank you also to everyone who crowdsourced this book! I am grateful for your belief in me and your support for this book to come to fruition!

Aaron Avery, Alex Tickle, Alexis Shepperd, Ali Berlin, Alicia Dattner, Alicia Davon, Alisha Musicant, Alyce DeChant, Alyssa Morin, Amy Weinberg, Andrew Finkelstein, Anjali Sawhney, Ann Greenwald, Boysen Hodgson, Brannon Hitt, Brenda Epperly, Brian Lenius, Brian Tubin, Bryan Bayer, Callie Miller, Caroline Boussenot, Catherine Wood, Charlie Rebich, Chris Kosley, Christie Bemis, Cleve Gaddis, Colin Rognlie, Dan Ancona, Dan Dore, Daniel Fritsch, Darrin Henderson, Dave Meader, David Wood, Demuse, DK Hyde, Edward Wargula, Eli Parker, Ellice Apostolos, Elliot Block, Emily Frazer, Eric Plumb, Erin Hanson, Erin Keeley, Evelyn Birnbaum, Frauhim Melblau, Frederick Polgardy, Gina Phillips, Glen Hun, Greg Tredo, Harry Silverstein, Heather Fink, Herbert Newman, Iris and Ken Weinstein, Iryna Melnykov, J. Mateson, James Baker, James Dial, James Lorr, Jamie Stark, Jeanine Becker, Jed Diamond, Jen Derwingson, Jennifer Sebastian, Jennifer Ciplet, Jessica Libbey, Jill Stein, Joe Bernstein, Joe Bilman, Joe Martinelli, Johanna Silver, John

Lewandowski, John Migliaccio, Joni Kozdeba, Joui Turandot, Juan Pablo Montúfar, Junie Moon Schreiber, Justin Smith, Kat Linquist, Kate Niebauer, Katherine fmw, Kevin Kerley, Kevin Waldman, Kim Arnold, Kristin Ertel, Kysha Mitchell, Lance Ingram, Laura Wald, Leslie Saglio, Lorn Dittfeld, Malissa Bullock, Marc Beneteau, Margaret O'Driscoll, Mark Siple, Matt Maxwell, Matthew Epsky, Megan Walrod, Meghan Neeley, Micah Weinberg, Michael David Sasson, Michael Ledford, Michael McGuinnes, Michael Neeley, Michael Porcelli, Michael Roesslein, Michael Welp, Naomi Benator, Neil Sattin, Neri Life Choma, Nicholas Jones, Nicola Persky, Nikki Pava, Ocean Robbins, Pamela Jay, Paul Arnold, Paul Augood, Randy Austill, Randy G., Ray Brejcha, Reginald Bulkley, Rivka Adini, Rob LaPlante, Robert Georges, Sage Lavine, Samantha Sweetwater, Sandra Lewis, Sarah Marshank, Scott Carroll, Sean Harvey, Sean Smith, Shannon Fisher, Shari Silk, Shelly Birger, Steve Berkwitz, Steven Lafond, Steven McGraw, Suiko McCall, Susan Campbell, Susannah Williams, Suzanne Quentin, Tery Elliot, Theresa Kepple, Thomas Edwards Jr, Timothy James, Tony Cooper, Tysen Bang, Velina Taneva, Viviana Lahrs, Wouter Slegers, and Zach Lawryk.

APPENDIX

INTRODUCTION

Wilcox, Bradford W. "The Evolution of Divorce." *National Affairs.* Accessed January 2022. https://www.nationalaffairs.com/publications/detail/the-evolution-of-divorce.

CHAPTER 1

DeBotton, Alain. "Why You Will Marry the Wrong Person." *New York Times.* May 28, 2016. https://www.nytimes.com/2016/05/29/opinion/sunday/why-you-will-marry-the-wrong-person.html.

Gottman, John, Julie Gottman, and Joan Declaire. *10 Lessons to Transform Your Marriage.* New York: Harmony Books, 2006.

Planned Parenthood. "History of Sex Education in the U.S." Accessed on May 27, 2022. https://www.plannedparenthood.org/uploads/filer_public/da/67/da67fd5d-631d-438a-85e8-a446d90fd1e3/20170209_sexed_d04_1.pdf.

CHAPTER 2

Apell, Elizabeth. Class Schedule, January 1979. Orinda, CA: John F Kennedy University.

Merriam-Webster. "Honest." Accessed January 2, 2022. https://www.dictionary.com/browse/stability.

Miller, Christian. "The Virtue of Honesty Requires More Than Just Telling the Truth." Psyche Magazine. December 13, 2021. https://psyche.co/ideas/more-than-just-truth-telling-honesty-is-a-virtue-to-cultivate

Resnick, Stella. The Pleasure Zone: Why We Resist Good Feelings & How To Let Go And Be Happy. Newburyport: Conari Press, 1997.

Rosenberg, Marshall. Nonviolent Communication. Encinitas, CA: Puddle Dancer Press, 2022.

Wake Forest University. "Funding: The Science of Honest." Accessed August 22, 2021. https://honestyproject.philosophy.wfu.edu/rfp-the-science-of-honesty/

CHAPTER 3

Colier, Nancy. "Why Our Thoughts Are Not Real." September 27, 2013. https://nancycolier.com/2013/09/27/why-our-thoughts-are-not-real/.

Gottman, John, Julie Gottman, and Joan Declaire. *10 Lessons to Transform Your Marriage*. New York: Harmony Books, 2006.

IFS Institute. "The Internal Family Systems Model Outline." 2022. https://ifs-institute.com/resources/articles/internal-family-systems-model-outline.

Merzel, Dennis Genpo. *Big Mind Big Heart: Finding Your Way*. Chicago: Big Mind Publishing, 2007.

Merzel, Dennis Genpo. "Introducing Big Mind" *Tricycle*, Winter 2008. https://tricycle.org/magazine/introducing-big-mind/.

Real, Terry. *Fierce Intimacy: Standing Up to One Another with Love*. Louisville: Sounds True, 2018.

Tolle, Eckhart. *The Power of Now: A Guide to Spiritual Enlightenment*. Vancouver: Namaste Publishing, 1999.

CHAPTER 4

Turrell, Emma Reed. *Please Yourself: How to Stop People Pleading and Transform the Way You Live*. London: Fourth Estate, 2021.

Welwood, John. "Human Nature. Buddha Nature." By Tina Fossella. *Tricycle* (Spring 2011). https://tricycle.org/magazine/human-nature-buddha-nature/.

Whyte, David. *Consolations: The Solace, Nourishment and Underlying Meaning of Everyday Words*. Many Rivers Press, 2020.

CHAPTER 5

Jang, Jia. *Rejection Proof: How I Beat Fear and Became Invincible Through 100 Days of Rejection*. New York: Harmony Publishing, 2015.

Roberts, Nicole. "Emotional and Physical Pain Are Almost the Same—to Your Brain." *Forbes*. February 14, 2020.

CHAPTER 6

Anand, Margo. *The Art of Sexual Magic*. New York: TarcherPerigree, 1996.

Darozhkina, Natallia. "Emily Nagoski: Pleasure Is the Measure— Transcript." *Blinkist Magazine*. April 12, 2018. https://www.blinkist.com/magazine/posts/simplify-sex-emily-nagoski-pleasure-measure-great-sex-life-transcript?utm_source=cpp.

Gray, Jordan. "33 Ways to Have Sex Without an Erection." December 8, 2020. https://www.jordangrayconsulting.com/sex-without-an-erection/.

Lafayette Morehouse. "Homepage." Accessed June 6, 2022.
http://www.lafayettemorehouse.com/#:~:text=Lafayette%20Morehouse%20is%20
an%20intentional,in%20the%20form%20of%20courses.

Mcintosh, James. "Everything You Need to Know about Orgasms."
MedicalNewsToday. January 17, 2022.
https://www.medicalnewstoday.com/articles/232318#:~:text=bone%2C%20
seemingly%20disappearing.-,Orgasm,of%20around%2013%2D51%20seconds.

Mintz, Laurie. *Becoming Cliterate: Why Orgasm Equality Matters—And How to Get
It.* San Francisco: HarperOne, 2017.

Perel, Esther. "*The Secret to Desire in Long Term Relationships.*" Filmed November 21,
2014 at TEDconference. TED video.
https://www.ted.com/talks/esther_perel_the_secret_to_desire_in_a_long_term_
relationship?language=en.

Robinson, Marnia. *Cupid's Poisoned Arrow: From Habit to Harmony in Sexual
Relationships.* Berkeley: North Atlantic Books, 2010.

Russer, Michael. "Impotence Could Be the Best Thing That Ever Happened to You."
April 15, 2020. In *Man Alive.* Podcast. MP3 audio.
https://shanajamescoaching.com/better-sex-life/.

Thomashauer, Regena. *Pussy: A Reclamation.* Carlsbad: Hay House, Inc., 2016.

Wade, Jenny. *Transcendent Sex: When Lovemaking Opens the Veil.* New York:
Gallery Books, 2004.

Wheal, Jamie. "Guerilla Tantra and the Sexual Yoga of Becoming." December 5, 2019.
In *Man Alive.* Podcast. MP3 audio.
https://shanajamescoaching.com/better-sex-life/.

CHAPTER 7

Bratton, Susan. "More Pleasure for Men." September 18, 2019. In *Man Alive.* Podcast.
MP3 audio.
https://shanajamescoaching.com/better-sex-life/.

Chia, Mantak. *The Alchemy of Sexual Energy: Connecting to the Universe from
Within.* Portland: Destiny Books, 2009.

Lafayette Morehouse. "Homepage." Accessed June 6, 2022.
http://www.lafayettemorehouse.com/#:~:text=Lafayette%20Morehouse%20is%20
an%20intentional,in%20the%20form%20of%20courses.

CHAPTER 8

Glover, Dr. Robert. *No More Mr. Nice Guy: A Proven Plan for Getting What You
Want in Love, Life and Sex.* Philadelphia: Running Press, 2010.

Handler, Laurie. *Sex and Happiness: The Tantric Laws of Intimacy.* Phoenix:
Butterfly Workshops Press, 2007.

Lewis, Sam Wren. *The Happiness Problem: Expecting Better in an Uncertain World.*
Bristol: Policy Press, 2019.

CHAPTER 9

Morin, Alyssa. "Simple Experiments for Better Sex." July 25, 2019. In *Man Alive*. Podcast. MP3 audio. https://shanajamescoaching.com/lovemaking2/

CHAPTER 10

Abrams, Douglas. *Book of Joy*. New Orleans: Cornerstone Digital, 2016.

Brackmann, Doug. "Harness the Power of a Type A Personality." September 20, 2021. In *Man Alive*. Podcast. MP3 audio. https://shanajamescoaching.com/better-sex-life/.

Dubois, Cleo. "Cléo Demonstrates Negotiation Skills." Accessed June 10, 2022. Video. https://www.youtube.com/watch?v=j1AscBJG9ew.

Goodreads. "Lao Tzu: Quotable Quotes." Accessed June 6, 2022. https://www.goodreads.com/quotes/8203490-watch-your-thoughts-they-become-your-words-watch-your-words.

Medcalf, Abby. "The Real Reasons Relationships Fail." Filmed September 24, 2021. TEDxOneonta. https://www.youtube.com/watch?v=KeeWRg_TofE.

Psaris, Jett, and Marlena Lyons. *Undefended Love*. Oakland: New Harbinger Publications, 2000.

Wheal, Jamie. "Guerilla Tantra and the Sexual Yoga of Becoming." December 5, 2019. In Man Alive. Podcast. MP3 audio. https://shanajamescoaching.com/better-sex-life/.

CHAPTER 11

Lewis, Mark Michael. *RelationDancing: Consciously Creating What You Really Want in Your Relating*. Greensboro: Life By Design Institute, 2003.

Rhett, Ian. "From Vision to Done: The CPR, a Tool That Keeps the 'Why' Up Front." February 2, 2016. https://www.linkedin.com/pulse/from-vision-done-cpr-tool-keeps-why-up-front-ian-rhett/

FINAL THOUGHTS

IFS Institute. "The Internal Family Systems Model Outline." 2022. https://ifs-institute.com/resources/articles/internal-family-systems-model-outline

Welwood, John. *Love and Awakening: The Sacred Path of Intimate Relationship*. New York: Harper Perennial, 1997.

ADDITIONAL RESOURCES

Additional resources from the experts in this book:

Alain de Botton
Why You Will Marry the Wrong Person Talk:
https://www.youtube.com/watch?v=-EvvPZFdjyk

Drs. John and Julie Gottman
Eight Dates
The 7 Principles for Making Marriage Work

Marshall Rosenberg
Nonviolent Communication: A Language of Life: Life-Changing Tools for Healthy Relationships

Susan Campbell
Getting Real
Five Minute Relationship Repair

Viktor Frankl
Man's Search for Meaning

Richard Schwartz
No Bad Parts: Healing Trauma and Restoring Wholeness with the Internal Family Systems Model

Sarah Marshank
Redefining Being Self-ish: My Journey from Escort to Monk to Grandmother
Selfistry: A Guide to Embodying Timeless Spiritual Wisdom

Terry Real
Us: Getting Past You & Me to Build a More Loving Relationship
I Don't Want to Talk About It: Overcoming the Secret Legacy of Male Depression

Shirzad Chamine
Positive Intelligence: Why Only 20% of Teams and Individuals Achieve Their True Potential and How You Can Achieve Yours

Marcia Baczynski
Creating Consent Culture

Osho
From Sex to Superconsciousness

Esther Perel
Mating in Captivity

Human Awareness Institute
https://www1.hai.org/

Body Electric
https://bodyelectric.org/

Susan Bratton
*Sexual Soulmates: The Six Essentials for Connected Sex
Relationship Magic*

Dr. Robert Glover
*Dating Essentials for Men: The Only Dating Guide You Will
Ever Need*

David Whyte
The Three Marriages

Cleo Dubois
https://www.cleodubois.com/

What 1000 Men's Tears Reveal About the Crisis Between
Men and Women
https://shanajamescoaching.com/tedx/

Man Alive podcast
https://shanajamescoaching.com/man-alive-podcast/

36 Questions for Deeper Intimacy:
https://shanajamescoaching.com/36-questions-for-deeper-
intimacy/

Made in the USA
Las Vegas, NV
10 August 2023

75919104R00138